Now I Get It

Now I Get It

Strategies for Building

Confident and Competent

Mathematicians, K–6

SUSAN O'CONNELL

HEINEMANN
Portsmouth, NH

Heinemann

A division of Reed Elsevier Inc.
361 Hanover Street
Portsmouth, NH 03801–3912
www.heinemann.com

Offices and agents throughout the world

Library of Congress Cataloging-in-Publication Data
O'Connell, Susan.
    Now I get it : strategies for building confident and competent mathematicians,
K–6 / Susan O'Connell.
        p.   cm.
    Includes bibliographical references.
    ISBN 0-325-00766-7 (alk. paper)
    1. Mathematics—Study and teaching (Elementary)—United States.   I. Title.
QA135.6.029   2005
372.7—dc22

                                                                2005008243

Editor: Victoria Merecki
Production: Elizabeth Valway
Cover and interior photography: Susan O'Connell
Cover design: Night & Day Design
Composition: Publishers' Design and Production Services, Inc.
Manufacturing: Louise Richardson

Printed in the United States of America on acid-free paper
09   08   07   06   05   ML   1   2   3   4   5

Contents

ON THE CD-ROM

Appendices—Practical Classroom Resources

A Sample Strategy Problems

B Activities to Review Basic Math Facts and Computation Skills

C Manipulative Templates

D Children's Literature Related to Math Concepts

E Math Vocabulary Lists

F Word Boxes

G Bingo Cards

H Math Writing Tasks

I Rubrics

J Graphic Organizers

K Math Centers

L "Must-See" Math Websites

To my husband, Pat
for his patience and continued support

Acknowledgments

A fundamental objective of this book is to promote reflection about teaching mathematics. Throughout my career, I have been influenced by a variety of professionals who have stimulated my thoughts about teaching and learning, including: Marilyn Burns, Thomas Carpenter, Randall Charles, Spencer Kagan, Steven Leinwand, Frank Lester, Robert Marzano, Jean Kerr Stenmark, John Van de Walle, and David Whitin. The research, insights, observations, and activities developed by these professionals have changed the way in which I think about mathematics teaching and learning.

The development of this book would not have been possible without the support and assistance of a variety of people. I am deeply grateful to the many teachers who have shared their insights with me, to the students who have challenged my thinking, and to my friends and colleagues who have provided me with continued assistance and encouragement.

Through observing students as they learn mathematics and through analyzing their work, we are able to gain tremendous insight into students' mathematical thinking. I am grateful to the students and teachers who welcomed me into their classrooms and shared their insights and understandings with me as I prepared this book. Thanks to the following students who contributed work samples or allowed their photographs to be taken for this book: Mark Anderson, Matthew Binder, Savannah Boyd, Cora Bradley, Alexandra Brunell, Skyler Chaplain, Kevin Conway, Alex DeBlauw, Caroline Dering, Joey DiGiacinto, Lisa Donn, Allison Fortney, Zachary Fraber, Maxwell Haffner, Kenneth Hagins, Summer Hall, Derek Harless, Kevin Hudgins, Kyre Hunte, Jorge Lainez, Nicole Lanton, Yemi Magbade, Erica Maletic, Jacen Martin, Marcus Maxwell, Connor McPeake, Jason Moeder, Megan Morley, Gideon Njoroge, Kajal Patel, Tara Pergerson, Argiro Potiris, Kristoffer Recio, Matthew Reilly, Sam Reinhart, Steven Rigby, Britni Ruff, Nancy Sanjines, Joshua Sharp, Imani Simpkins, Autumn Sims, Rachelle Tompkins, Khalil Wiggins, Dennis Witol, and Madison Young. And thank you to the following teachers who either welcomed me into their classrooms to conduct lessons, shared student work samples, or allowed me to take photographs in their classrooms: Jennifer Beyea, Pat Donofrio, Liz Finnerty, Nikki Friedland, Desiree Hoke, Anne McLaughlin, Brendan O'Connell, Katie O'Connell, Ruth Richman, and Cheryl Vincent.

I would like to extend my gratitude to my colleagues who provided feedback or assisted me in collecting resource information. Thanks to Stacey Williams, Kelly O'Connor, Gail Naworal, and Susan Denvir—colleagues at the University of Maryland who provided feedback on specific chapters. Stacey Williams' expertise in differentiating instruction, Kelly O'Connor's knowledge of reading and literature techniques, Gail Naworal's extensive experience with parent involvement programs, and Susan Denvir's understanding of cooperative learning strategies were extremely helpful in refining those chapters. I would also like to thank the teachers who provided thoughtful feedback on specific chapters: Leila Dowdall, Liz Finnerty, Ann Hefflin, Colleen Klemens, and Katie O'Connell. Their practical experience and knowledge of sound instructional strategies were invaluable. Thanks also to Joanie Pinson for her research on children's literature and to Jason King for sharing his technology expertise.

Thank you to Donna Wiseman, Associate Dean for Teacher Education in the College of Education at the University of Maryland, for her understanding in adjusting my responsibilities to allow me to dive fully into this project.

Many thanks to Victoria Merecki, my Heinemann editor, for her patience and encouragement, and for answering the many questions that were thrown her way during the preparation of this manuscript.

Most especially, thank you to my family, my husband, Pat, and my children, Brendan and Katie, for dealing with my many hours at the computer while writing and rewriting this book. I am deeply grateful for their understanding and support throughout the entire process.

Introduction

As we look back on our experiences as students in the math classroom, many of us summon memories of quietly sitting in straight rows, working diligently on paper-and-pencil tasks. Silently, we practiced our calculation skills. If anything was heard in the classroom, it was our teacher's voice, telling us the right way—the one way—to do these calculations. Our job was to practice until we could do it *right*, and "right" was measured by our ability to get the correct answer. Some students excelled at the calculations and were rewarded with excellent math grades. Some even had an understanding of the processes, being able to later apply their skills to problem solving. For those who were able to master the calculation processes, a feeling of competence emerged. But for those who struggled with manipulating the numbers or with understanding the math concepts embedded in the processes, frustration, anxiety, and a feeling of incompetence were imminent. Some students became convinced that they could not do math. Others thought they could do math, only to find out later that they were unable to apply their skills to problem-solving tasks. Many students within those classrooms turned away from math, often at a very young age.

Although there is no doubt that many of us thrived in traditional classrooms, we now recognize that there were many others who became frustrated and anxious because of their inability to grasp the concepts. While some students seemed to know the answer the instant the teacher posed the question, others were still processing the question as the teacher moved on to the next problem. As a classroom teacher, I often sat across the table from my students' parents at conference times and was astounded by how many of them expressed negative feelings about their own math skills and abilities. These adults clearly articulated their low self-concept about math skills, as well as their dislike for mathematics as a result of their experiences. Such parents were the students who had been turned-off to math years before, who had been made to feel as though they could not learn math and that math was for a few people with special skills and abilities. Math for all students was not reflective of their classroom experiences.

Throughout the country, many of our teachers attempted to teach math to diverse groups of learners in one formulaic approach—an approach that was effective for some but did not reach countless others. Today's goal is to find instructional techniques that support all students in their understanding of mathematics—techniques that offer students opportunities to explore mathematics; talk about understandings; visualize complex thinking; and, ultimately, apply math to real tasks. We have been challenged to uncover instructional techniques to help all students understand the math they will need throughout their lives.

About This Book

This book addresses the art of teaching mathematics. It is a compilation of powerful instructional strategies that are meant to enhance the teaching of math content. The highlighted strategies provide teachers with options for assisting all students in constructing an understanding of math concepts. The instructional strategies are aligned with the National Council of Teachers of Mathematics' standards (NCTM 1989, NCTM 1991, NCTM 2000) and provide engaging and motivating ways to teach mathematics to elementary students. An accompanying CD provides ready-to-use resources. Topics include the role of manipulatives, discourse, writing, demonstrations, and cooperative learning to help students build conceptual understandings. Instructional ideas for assisting students with mastering basic skills and developing mathematical thinking are presented. The use of children's literature as a springboard to math teaching, and strategies to differentiate instruction to meet the needs of all learners are addressed. Techniques to assess student understanding are presented, as well as ideas for increasing parental involvement. This book provides research, resources, and practical ideas for teaching mathematics to all students.

Becoming an Effective Teacher of Mathematics

Becoming an effective teacher of mathematics unquestionably requires a thorough understanding of math content. However, we have all known teachers who were brilliant mathematicians, yet ineffective teachers. The effective teacher of mathematics blends content knowledge with an ability to deliver that content so that others understand it. Quality teaching requires mathematics knowledge and instructional skills. In *Principles and Standards for School Mathematics* (2000), the National Council of Teachers of Mathematics (NCTM) clarified the content that should be addressed in math classrooms; students need to understand numbers and operations, algebra, geometry, measurement, and data analysis and probability in order to have a balanced understanding of mathematics. NCTM's standards encourage teachers to incorporate the processes of reasoning, problem solving, communication, connections, and representations into all math instruction.

It is these processes that help students understand the mathematics content they are studying; and, it is through these processes that we are able to bring mathematical understanding to all students.

Even this critical blend of content knowledge and instructional skill is not enough to be an effective mathematics teacher. To be an effective teacher, one has to have a passion for what he or she teaches. To demonstrate that passion for math and nurture a love of math within our students, we must exhibit a positive attitude toward mathematics. This can be difficult for the teacher who struggled with math as a student and still remembers the associated anxiety or frustration. As I collaborate with practicing teachers, they continually remark about their early experiences with mathematics and the impact those experiences have had on their current attitudes. However, I also have been privileged to witness the reshaping of these attitudes about mathematics as teachers begin to teach in new ways. As they add new instructional techniques to their repertoire and witness how they impact their students' understanding, I hear remarks like the following: "Why didn't someone show me this years ago?" "I really enjoy math now!" "I would have understood this if I had been taught this way!" "NOW, I get it!"

Focusing on Understanding and Application

We recognize the importance of computational skills, but also now recognize that an understanding of mathematics and the application of math skills are equally important in the development of competent mathematicians. Our goal is to find instructional practices to enlighten students about math concepts; practices that will assist them in applying both calculation skills and reasoning skills to real math problems, as well as spark an interest in further study.

As we reflect on past practices, we strive to modify our teaching so that it encompasses the basic skills, the development of conceptual understanding about mathematics, and the ability to apply both calculation and reasoning skills to problem situations. The inclusion of discourse and writing in our math classrooms has opened the door to opportunities to help students see our thinking and to try some thinking of their own. The use of manipulatives has allowed students to explore math concepts in a hands-on way to develop a better understanding of them. The use of flexible grouping has allowed us to differentiate instruction to meet the needs of a variety of learners. A focus on problem solving has facilitated connecting calculations to the reason for learning them—to solve problems. The move toward partner and group work has allowed students to share ideas and to learn from the ideas of others. The emphasis on real-world connections and teaching math in context has allowed us to show the meaningfulness of math topics. The use of technology resources has helped us to support and advance student learning. The welcoming of parental involvement has allowed us to cultivate student learning both in school and at home. Instructional practices to enrich students' understanding of mathematics and to develop their capabilities in using the math they are learning are discussed throughout this book.

Reflecting on Our Beliefs About Mathematics

When first teaching mathematics, I was unaware of the strong influence of my experiences on my teaching style and techniques. I taught math the way I had been taught math. I had developed a system of beliefs about mathematics based on my experiences and observations as a student. As a teacher of mathematics, I began to question those beliefs as I struggled to find ways to help my students understand mathematics. I have been continually amazed at the number of teachers I encounter who developed similar beliefs and struggled, as I did, to change those beliefs to improve their instructional skills. The following sections describe my ten (misinformed) beliefs about mathematics. As I began to question these beliefs, I was able to modify my teaching of mathematics.

Misinformed Belief 1—Practice Makes Perfect

I am convinced that my teachers heartily believed this. I can clearly remember pages of calculations that took entire class periods to complete. If there were 50 problems on the worksheet, we had to do all 50. This practice-makes-perfect attitude was just one of many that we embraced without argument as we quietly worked in the math classroom. Convinced that the more we did, the better at math we would become, we endured long lists of calculations until the process became automatic!

As I made decisions about the assignments I gave to my students, I began to wonder whether the quality of the exercises shouldn't be more important than the quantity. On that page of 50 problems, could I assign numbers 1 to 5, then 15 to 20, then 35 to 40? Would students still master the process? Would they do the problems without becoming bored and careless in their work? Does repeated practice ensure understanding?

Misinformed Belief 2—Mastering Calculations Is the Ultimate Goal

The majority of my time in the math classroom was spent learning calculations. My teachers stayed on certain chapters (long division comes to mind) for inordinate amounts of time until everyone had mastered the process. If we didn't get to the geometry chapter, skipped measurement this year, or cut out the word problems at the end of the pages, it was okay because we had mastered those calculations. Year after year, my teachers skimped on the same topics, giving me a narrow view of mathematics. Should calculations be taught to the exclusion of other strands of mathematics? Is mastery always necessary? What is the role of revisiting concepts frequently to improve and refine students' skills? Is presenting a balance of math concepts essential for developing well-rounded mathematicians?

Misinformed Belief 3—Math Is About Getting the Right Answer

I spent all of my K–12 years believing this. After all, the answer was the only thing evaluated—it was right or wrong; there was no gray area in math. Once I began to teach math and to reevaluate my thoughts about mathematics, I began to wonder if the thinking shouldn't be as important as the answer. Is the answer an adequate way to assess math understanding? Is a correct answer more important than a correct math process? Does a correct answer always indicate conceptual understanding?

Misinformed Belief 4—Math Is a Series of Isolated Skills

My mathematics classes were about completing a series of isolated skills. Each year, we would progress through the book, studying what I thought was a series of unrelated math topics. We learned to add two-digit numbers, then took a test. We learned to measure length, then took a test. Then we learned the names and characteristics of shapes, and took a test. Skills and concepts were taught in isolation, with few connections between them. I was assessed on my ability to add fractions; the connection between fractions, decimals, and percents was not explored. Is mathematics a series of isolated skills? Does understanding connections between mathematical skills and processes improve students' understanding?

Misinformed Belief 5—You Must Know Basic Skills Before You Can Learn to Solve Problems

Instruction in math had a definite sequence. We memorized and practiced math facts until they were mastered. Then, we learned basic computations. Finally, we moved to problem solving. It was about the basics, then the thinking skills. Computations were on the top of the page and a few problems were at the bottom. Some days we never made it to the problems at the bottom of the page because we hadn't yet mastered the calculations. As I watch primary students reason through mathematics concepts, I wonder how many opportunities were missed by my teachers holding students back because of memorization difficulties. Can students continue to practice basic facts while developing thinking skills? Does an inability to memorize mean one has an inability to do other math processes? Should problem solving be an endpoint to instruction? Or, should problems be posed as an introduction to learning calculation skills to motivate students and set the context for their learning?

Misinformed Belief 6—First One Finished Wins

I remember racing through calculations to be the first one to hand in the paper or to raise my hand to show I had finished. Speed was important. After all, we raced to see who could blurt out a flash-card answer first or beat another student when doing a calculation at the blackboard. Everyone learned that speed was a valued quality. Do we have students who can calculate the answers, but struggle to get the solutions quickly? Are we sending a message that speed is more important than ability? Is the goal speed or accuracy?

Misinformed Belief 7—The Best Mathematicians Can Work Calculations in Their Heads

We were in awe of those students who could quickly calculate answers "in their heads." They couldn't tell us how they got the answer, and we didn't really care. We were so impressed that they got the answer, and without using any paper! My teacher's praise of those students led me to believe that doing it in an abstract way was better than the paper-and-pencil way. Should we always solve problems in our heads? When might we need to *see* our thinking with a quick paper-and-pencil sketch or a concrete representation? Should that method be valued less? Is it possible that some students excel at abstract methods while others are very capable when allowed to use visual or concrete methods?

Misinformed Belief 8—Teachers Should Tell Us How to Do Math

My teachers told us how to do math. They showed us step by step how to figure out the answer. They gave lectures and demonstrated processes, then checked to be sure we were doing it in the way they had taught us. I did not actively develop understandings through exploration. I did not discover formulas through investigations. Is the math teacher's job to tell students how and what to do? Can a teacher guide students' development through questioning rather than telling? Is it possible for teachers to support students as they discover mathematics' concepts?

Misinformed Belief 9—Math Is Done Just in Math Class

Mathematics was a subject in school. For my friends who struggled in high school math, they took solace in the fact that they would only need to take it a couple more years and then they would be done. Forever! Is math more than a subject in school? Do students see the connection to their lives? Are students able to extract what they have learned in math class so that it becomes a usable tool in their lives?

Misinformed Belief 10—Some Are Good at Math, Some Are Not

I believed that there were those who could do math and those who couldn't. We were all given the same lecture or demonstration and some of us got it and some didn't. That certainly proved the point! I judged whether students were able to learn it without considering the ways in which they were taught math. Can all students learn math? Do students build understanding and make sense of mathematics in different ways? Should varied instructional techniques be used routinely in the math classroom? Is it a teacher's responsibility to search for alternate methods of teaching math skills and concepts so that all students have an opportunity to learn regardless of their preferred learning styles?

In reflecting on my misconceptions about mathematics, I was able to discover exciting alternatives to the traditional teaching of math that I had experienced, alternatives that motivated and engaged students and maximized their achievement. Questioning my misinformed beliefs allowed me to gain a greater understanding of mathematics and unearth ways to help my students develop their mathematical understandings.

How This Book Can Help You

Many elementary teachers recognize the mathematics they experienced is not the mathematics they want their students to experience. While we understand the reasons for change, it is often difficult to figure out *how* to change. We become caught in a cycle of teaching in the way in which we were taught. This book offers a doable approach to change. Through reflecting on research-based instructional strategies and combining this reflection with practical, classroom-tested ideas, teachers have a road map for creating the kind of classroom that they wish they had experienced as students.

Some districts view textbook selection as the way to improve math instruction; however, this book looks to the improvement of teachers' skills as a more basic approach that yields a more lasting impact. It is teachers who select tasks and resources, manage discourse, analyze learning, and create the learning environment (NCTM 1991)—no textbook can do that. Quality teaching is a reflection of being able to make effective instructional decisions that enhance learning for our students.

As we struggle to shift our instruction from a teacher-centered, answer-driven approach to a student-centered, inquiry-based approach, we yearn for ideas, support, assurance, and suggestions to help make this change attainable. This book provides the framework for putting change within your reach. It is meant to be used as a starting point for the journey to change, which can happen in small steps. Whether you are a novice or a veteran, you will find a variety of ideas to allow you to reflect on your current practices and choose strategies that will work with your style, your textbook, and your students.

As a practical handbook for teachers of mathematics, this book provides a wealth of ideas for engaging, motivating, and teaching students in elementary math classrooms. You might choose to read it from start to finish, or to explore specific chapters as the content sparks your interest or addresses your needs. Like any handbook, it is intended to serve as an ongoing resource as you plan, deliver, and assess mathematics' lessons throughout the year. The best practices highlighted in the chapters that follow emanate from experts in the field of education as well as practicing teachers throughout the country. They are classroom-tested approaches grounded in educational research.

In each chapter, instructional techniques are described, and practical tips are shared, to assist you in implementing the techniques within your classroom. The materials on the CD-ROM are meant as support for busy educators by providing a myriad of resources so that you can easily implement the techniques. The chapters are organized to provide you with a rationale for the instructional practices, and there are student work samples to illustrate ideas. Questions, which can be used for self-reflection or as discussion starters for study groups or school meetings, are included. Each chapter also contains a list of suggested texts and video resources to support and guide your professional development, because enhancing instructional skills is an ongoing process.

Summary

This book is a practical handbook for teachers of mathematics. It provides ideas, activities, and resources to engage teachers in reflection about teaching, as well as suggested tools to enhance teaching. As you read, reflect on your beliefs about mathematics, your experiences learning and teaching mathematics, and your observations of your students' successes and frustrations as they explore mathematics. Our goal is to design our classrooms as places where involvement in mathematical discourse and exploration can lead students to a true understanding of math concepts; to design classrooms as places where we can develop confident and competent mathematicians and nurture a love of math within our students.

Questions for Reflection

1. What were your experiences as a student in the math classroom? What teaching techniques do you recall? Were those techniques effective for you? Were they effective for everyone in your class?
2. Did you develop any beliefs about mathematics based on your experiences and observations? Have you modified those beliefs as a result of your teaching experiences?
3. Do you believe that it is difficult for a teacher to break the habit of teaching in the way in which he or she was taught? Why or why not?
4. What obstacles make it difficult to teach in a new way? How might someone overcome those obstacles?
5. Do you see evidence within your classroom that students thrive on a variety of instructional strategies?
6. Do you have a preferred method of instructional delivery? Are there other instructional techniques you would like to develop? What support would you need to fully incorporate those techniques into your teaching repertoire?

Suggested Resources

Carpenter, Thomas P., and Thomas A. Romberg. 2004. *Powerful Practices in Mathematics and Science*. Madison: The Board of Regents of the University of Wisconsin (CD-ROM and monograph).

National Council of Teachers of Mathematics. 1989. *Curriculum and Evaluation Standards for School Mathematics*. Reston, VA: National Council of Teachers of Mathematics.

———. 1991. *Professional Standards for Teaching Mathematics*. Reston, VA: National Council of Teachers of Mathematics.

———. 2000. *Principles and Standards for School Mathematics*. Reston, VA: National Council of Teachers of Mathematics.

Rowan, Thomas, and Barbara Bourne. 2001. *Thinking Like Mathematicians: Putting the NCTM Standards into Practice*. Portsmouth, NH: Heinemann.

Staff Development Training Videos

Burns, Marilyn. 2002. *Mathematics Teaching for Understanding*. Vernon Hills, IL: ETA/Cuisenaire.

Now I Get It

CHAPTER ONE

Problem Solving as the Focus of Math Instruction

Why is there so much attention on math problem solving? And, why does this book begin with a discussion of problem solving? A reasonable question since as a student of mathematics I clearly remember computational activities coming before problem-solving activities. First we learned computations, then we solved problems. But beginning with problem solving seems to me to be the perfect way to start this book. Today, we recognize problem solving as the central focus of the math curriculum (NCTM 1989). It is the reason why we teach students to add, subtract, multiply, and divide; to work with decimals, fractions, and percents; to navigate through measurement and geometry. It is what makes all of these isolated skills make sense, and it is what gives purpose to teaching them. In the math classrooms of the past, problem solving was an add-on. It was what we did at the end of a lesson when we solved a couple related word problems or what we did at the end of a chapter that had focused primarily on computations. Today, we view its role as central to teaching mathematics.

What Is Math Problem Solving?

Problem solving is both a method of teaching and a skill to be taught. Problem solving is an approach to teaching mathematics in which students engage in problem situations in order to explore and develop understanding of mathematical concepts. It is also a set of thinking skills or strategies that, when developed, helps students solve mathematical tasks. It is important to teach both through problem solving and about problem solving (Van de Walle 2004).

Problem solving is a complex and critical topic in mathematics education. This book discusses both problem-centered instruction and the teaching of problem-solving strategies. Problem-centered instruction provides students with opportunities to explore their thinking and computational skills. Such explorations set the stage for understanding algorithms (Van de Walle 2004, Fennema and Romberg 1999). Problems are posed through which students are challenged to find solutions. Often, students use their intuitive knowledge to solve problems even before they are taught specific math skills. Problem-centered instruction generally leads to the development of computational skills, and because these skills are developed through a problem-solving context, students truly understand the skills. Through problem-centered instruction, students are empowered with finding solutions and gaining insights through explorations that require them to use the math skills and strategies they possess or to invent their own strategies to help them find solutions.

In addition, many students benefit from guidance in developing strategies that help them experience success during problem-solving activities. These thinking strategies help students organize information, recognize relationships between numbers, effectively draw conclusions, and provide a path to move toward a solution. Modeling, class discussions, and focused lessons on developing thinking skills greatly benefit students and move them forward in their ability to become effective problem solvers. Both aspects of problem solving are discussed in this chapter, with the understanding that students benefit from a variety of approaches for the teaching of problem solving including problem-centered explorations and discussions and activities related to the development of problem-solving strategies.

Teaching mathematics through a problem-centered approach, combined with a focus on understanding critical problem-solving strategies, is a sound instructional plan for building strong and effective problem solvers.

Why Focus on Problem Solving?

Problem-solving experiences focus students on mathematical understanding rather than on isolated, rote computations. They challenge students to connect mathematical ideas, to apply skills to problem situations, to employ thinking skills to organize and analyze data, and to use communication and reflection skills to make sense of mathematical ideas. Problem-solving experiences, in which students must find an answer and then develop a way to clearly share that answer with others, support the development of mathematical understanding (Hiebert et al. 1997, Lester and Charles 2003). Problem-solving activities focus students on the core of the mathematics curriculum.

Problem solving engages students in *doing* mathematics; they are actively involved when solving problems. Problem-solving activities stimulate students' curiosity and involve them in explorations and discussions that give meaning to the math skills they are learning. Problem solving motivates students to explore math ideas. Problem solving is fun!

Problem-solving activities develop students' inquiry skills (Whitin and Cox 2003). The development of thinking and reasoning skills is critical in that it provides students with the tools to gather new insights and to continue to develop their understandings (NCTM 2000). As students hone their problem-solving skills, they are better able to explore new math challenges and face more complex tasks.

Teaching problem-solving strategies and engaging students in problem explorations help them learn to organize their thinking, and it teaches them various methods for finding solutions. Effective problem solvers are aware of how they solve problems and know how to monitor and adjust their strategies to move toward solutions (Bransford, Brown, and Cocking 1999). Problem-solving activities, and reflections about those activities, teach students to recognize their own ways of thinking and help to expand their repertoire of thinking skills.

Positive problem-solving experiences build students' confidence in their ability to do math. Students gain confidence in their own skills and learn to respect the skills and insights of others as they work together to solve problems. Problem solving generates pride in accomplishment and provides students with opportunities to learn to work with and listen to others' ideas—it promotes collaboration.

Observing and assessing students' problem-solving experiences allows teachers to determine whether students understand math skills, as well as how effectively they can apply skills and concepts to problem situations. As students explain and justify solutions or processes, teachers are able to see their level of understanding and whether they can apply ideas. This assessment information provides critical insights to drive instructional decision making.

Finally, the critical-thinking skills developed, as students explore, discuss, and reflect on problem situations, provides a strong foundation for the understanding of many higher-level mathematics' concepts. As students recognize and extend patterns, or analyze the relationships between numbers in tables, they are building foundational skills that will support their understanding of algebraic concepts. The use of diagrams and the application of logical reasoning skills will enhance students' understanding of geometry. As students reflect on their own thinking (metacognition), they become better able to identify how they make decisions about appropriate strategies and how they reassess their efforts and shift gears when a solution is not readily apparent. Opportunities to face increasingly more complex problem situations that require thoughtful approaches and extensive effort help to nurture a strong problem-solving attitude, which will prove vital as students move into more sophisticated mathematical topics.

What Is Problem-Centered Instruction?

Problem-centered instruction uses problems to launch math lessons. In problem-centered instruction, students are engaged in interesting and meaningful tasks that provide a context for discussions about math ideas. In solving the problems, students use their own

methods and teachers facilitate the sharing of ideas and reflections about students' insights and discoveries. Through problem-centered instruction, teachers select and introduce worthwhile tasks that promote understanding of math concepts, guide explorations, and help students pull ideas and understanding from the activities.

Van de Walle (2004) describes the teacher's role in problem-centered instruction in a before/during/after format in which teachers set up the problem with clear directions and guidelines prior to the task as well as possibly engaging students in a focusing activity to prepare them for the experience. During problem solving, students are allowed to follow their own paths as teachers listen to their ideas and processes, or provide hints or prompts to groups who require support. Following the task, teachers engage them in math talk about the problem-solving experience so that they can learn from each other as well as from their experiences. Teachers select the task, pose questions, facilitate group work, assist students in reflecting, and use their observations to assess students' understanding.

In problem-centered instruction, tasks should be carefully selected to promote student thinking. They should lend themselves to varied approaches as students explore the activity, and tasks should challenge them to use computation and reasoning skills. Primary students might be asked to figure out how many pieces of fruit could be in each bowl if there were 3 bowls and 8 pieces of fruit; they will use different strategies and find variety of answers. Even before they have the ability to add or to multiply to find answers, students will find other methods to determine the answer to problems as they draw pictures, represent the data with objects, or use their counting skills.

In Figures 1.1 and 1.2, fourth graders were asked to figure out how 4 quesadillas might be shared equally among 3 friends. The students solved the problem in different ways, but both methods showed an understanding of the

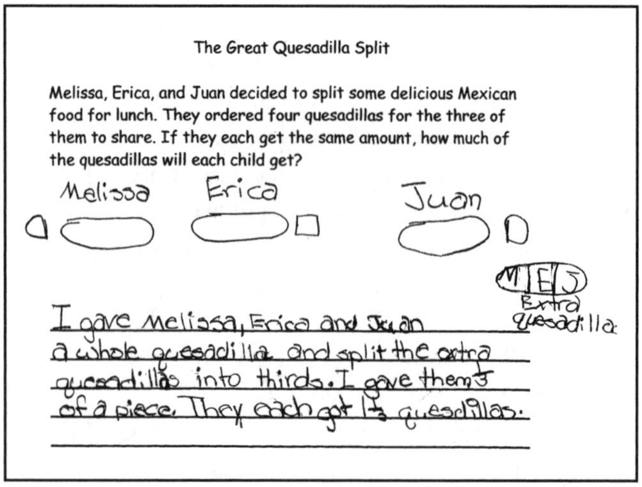

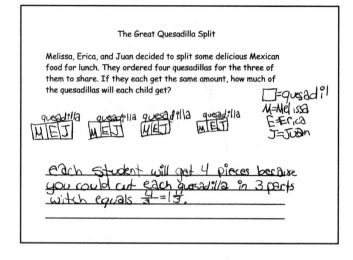

FIGURE 1.1 This student first gave each child a quesadilla and then split the remaining 1 between the 3 children to give everyone 1 $\frac{1}{3}$ quesadillas.

FIGURE 1.2 This student split each quesadilla into 3 parts and gave each child $\frac{1}{3}$ of each quesadilla. Each child received $\frac{4}{3}$ quesadillas.

mathematics in it. As they shared their different methods with the class, important concepts about fractions emerged.

Having discussions about the problem experience and the sharing of students' various problem-solving methods is a critical stage in problem-centered instruction. The teacher facilitates reflections by asking students "How?" and "Why?" and "What if . . . ?" The teacher encourages students to share conjectures, to defend answers, and to explain their thinking. Later chapters explore the role of whole-class discussions (Chapter 7), teacher questioning (Chapter 5), student-to-student talk (Chapter 7), and writing about mathematical ideas (Chapter 8) in more detail because of their key role in developing mathematical understanding. Understanding develops as a result of communication and reflection (Heibert et al. 1997).

The National Council of Teachers of Mathematics (2000) maintains that students should be able to "monitor and reflect on the process of mathematical problem solving (182)." In order to support students in their ability to reflect on problem-solving experiences and be able to identify and effectively talk about the ways in which they solve problems, discussions about problem-solving strate-

gies are essential. Discussing such thinking strategies allows students to better recognize their own thinking processes (metacognition).

What Does It Mean to Teach Problem-Solving Strategies?

While the NCTM (2000) states that all students should be able to construct new math ideas through problem-solving experiences (problem-centered instruction), it also emphasizes the importance of students being able to use and to adapt a variety of appropriate problem-solving strategies. Teaching about these problem-solving strategies is an important part of helping students develop as problem solvers. It is essential to clarify the term *teach* at the start of this discussion. When we talk about teaching fractions, we know that we do not mean simply telling students about fractions. To teach fractions, we use various approaches including investigations, discussions, and demonstrations. In the same way, when we teach problem-solving strategies, we are not implying a drill-and-practice approach to learning about these thinking skills. Like the teaching of any other math skill, the teaching of problem solving involves a variety of approaches so that students can see ideas modeled, experience situations, discuss insights and observations, and process learning through talking and writing. Students benefit from seeing problem-solving strategies modeled and from practice applying them to problem situations (Burns 1992a). Teaching problem-solving strategies is not about telling students which strategies to use.

Different students will have different needs for developing their use of problem-solving strategies. Many students are intuitive problem solvers and use problem-solving strategies effectively without ever being taught them. For such students, teaching problem-solving strategies may simply be helping them recognize the strategies they are using—giving a name to what is going on in their heads—so that they can talk about it and later apply it to more complex problems. For others, teaching problem-solving strategies may be a process of guiding them to discover a strategy or thinking skill that would make the problem simpler or more doable. It may involve demonstrating and modeling for some who are not coming up with the strategies on their own. Through visual demonstrations or hands-on experiences, students are often able to understand an otherwise abstract thinking skill and make it a part of their repertoire. Teaching problem-solving strategies is the process of helping students realize what they do as they solve problems as well as helping them discover ways they could do it more efficiently. In both cases, the teaching of problem-solving strategies requires a great deal of discussion and reflection, as ideas are shared, clarified, and refined.

Which Thinking Skills Are Essential to Be an Effective Problem Solver?

Through problem-solving instruction, we assist students in the development of critical thinking skills that will support their ability to tackle increasingly complex math problems. Carefully scaffolded questions, visual demonstrations, hands-on experiences, classroom discussions, and the sharing of solutions all help students identify problem-solving methods and develop a repertoire of problem-solving strategies. Focusing on the following strategies will help students develop a variety of important thinking skills.

> Choose an operation
> Find a pattern
> Make a table
> Make an organized list
> Draw a picture or diagram
> Guess, check, and revise
> Use logical reasoning
> Work backward

These terms seem quite simple to describe thought processes. The actual thinking skills required to be an effective problem solver are much more complex, but these briefer, more understandable terms can help students recognize their thinking processes so that they can verbalize what they are experiencing. By using simplified terms, even primary students can discuss thinking processes and how they organize ideas and make sense of the mathematics in a problem. As first graders talk about patterns they've noticed or third graders talk about making tables to organize data, they are speaking the language of problem solving.

Choose an Operation

Certainly choosing the correct operation and building appropriate equations is a critical problem-solving skill. Teachers have begun to focus more on the conceptual understanding of operations rather than just drilling rote facts; this provides a great foundation for helping students select appropriate strategies as they try to solve problems. Students who understand addition or multiplication are better able to recognize addition or multiplication scenarios as they encounter them in problems. However, while understanding operations is critical to being an effective problem solver, understanding operations alone is not enough to allow students to tackle the variety of problems they will encounter. It is important to help them expand their repertoire of strategies for solving problems so that they are prepared for the challenges they might face.

Find a Pattern

Being able to recognize and extend patterns is another critical problem-solving skill. Our number system is a system of patterns. In some cases, students can solve problems simply by recognizing patterns within data and by extending those patterns to find a solution. Engaging students in discussions about the patterns they see and displaying visuals using 100 Charts or number lines (see Appendix C) will help strengthen their ability to see a variety of patterns in mathematical situations.

Make a Table

Making tables provides students with a method for organizing data. When data is organized, students often can more easily see patterns or functional relationships within it. Discussions should center around the way that numbers within the table are connected. If primary students are asked to figure out how much 5 stickers would cost if 1 sticker costs 5 cents, a table may be a way to display the data so that they can see the cost as it increases by increments of 5. By viewing the data on a table, students see the pattern and are able to find the solution.

Cost of Stickers

Number of stickers	1	2	3	4	5
Cost (cents)	5	10	15	20	

Intermediate students might be asked to complete tables with more complicated numbers. Using the table, students are able to analyze the numbers to determine the missing data.

Cookie Ingredients per Batch

Sugar (cups)	2	4	6	8	10
Oil (cups)	$\frac{1}{3}$	$\frac{2}{3}$	1		$1\frac{2}{3}$

To find the missing value of $1\frac{1}{3}$ for column four, students might notice the horizontal pattern on the table (adding $\frac{1}{3}$) or might recognize the functional relationship that appears vertically (the cups of sugar is 6 times more than the cups of oil). Discussions should focus on students' observations and insights about the table's data and how they were able to complete it as a result of their observations.

Make an Organized List

Making organized lists focuses students' attention on two key ideas that often help them simplify problems: (1) organizing data and (2) recording data. Many students do not intuitively move through problems in organized and systematic ways and yet doing that usually simplifies problems. Typical problems for which this strategy would be beneficial are combination problems, such as one in which students are asked to find all of the sandwich/ drink combinations if they can have a turkey, tuna, or ham sandwich and milk or lemonade. Students often verbalize combinations in random order, so are unable to find all of the possibilities. The organized-list strategy helps students see that starting at a beginning point and moving systematically through the data, exhausting possibilities as they move along, will make the problem easier to solve.

In addition, this strategy encourages students to record through a list, and later a tree diagram. Recording information allows students to look back at what they've done and enables them to focus on the next step rather than trying to remember everything that has already been done. Students who use an organized list become confident that they did not miss possibilities, or mention combinations more than once, and feel more sure of their solutions.

Draw a Picture or Diagram

Through the use of pictures, diagrams, or manipulatives, students are able to show what they know about a problem and, once they have visualized it, are often better able to move toward a solution. Primary students might be asked to determine how many apples and bananas Katie had if she had 3 bags of fruit and there were 2 apples and 1 banana in each bag. A simple picture can help students visualize the situation and solve the problem (see Figure 1.3). Intermediate students might be challenged with determining Susie's age knowing that the top of her circular birthday cake has a ring of 8 roses and that between each rose are 2 candles. By drawing a diagram of the cake, students can more easily determine her age. Often abstract ideas are more difficult to work with and the act of just making the problem visual immediately simplifies the task. We can help students visualize problems by using real objects as models, or manipulatives, pictures, or diagrams to represent real things.

Guess, Check, and Revise

A frequently used problem-solving approach is trial and error. The guess, check, and revise strategy helps students identify this type of thinking. Number sense, a very important skill for understanding and using mathematics effectively, is an integral component of this strategy. Students need to make reasonable guesses and learn to revise them to get closer to an answer. Primary students might be asked to determine how Dan scored 6 points at a carnival by throwing 3 balls into cups. A ball in the blue cup scored 5 points, a ball in the red cup scored 3 points, a ball in the yellow cup scored 2 points, and a ball in the green cup scored 1 point. While there may be more than one answer (if more than one ball can be thrown in the same cup), all answers require an understanding of numbers. Discussions might focus on why Dan could not have thrown a ball in the blue cup or why all 3 balls could not have gone in the green cup. Intermediate students might be asked to determine which three consecutive pages Brendan read in his book if the sum of the page numbers was 72. Students need to use their understanding of numbers to begin with a reasonable guess and then revise the guess based on each trial.

Teacher think-aloud demonstrations are particularly helpful in sharing the thought process that goes on during guess, check, and revise thinking. Using think-alouds, teachers verbalize their thoughts as they model a reasonable first guess and as they demonstrate how to adjust guesses to work toward a solution.

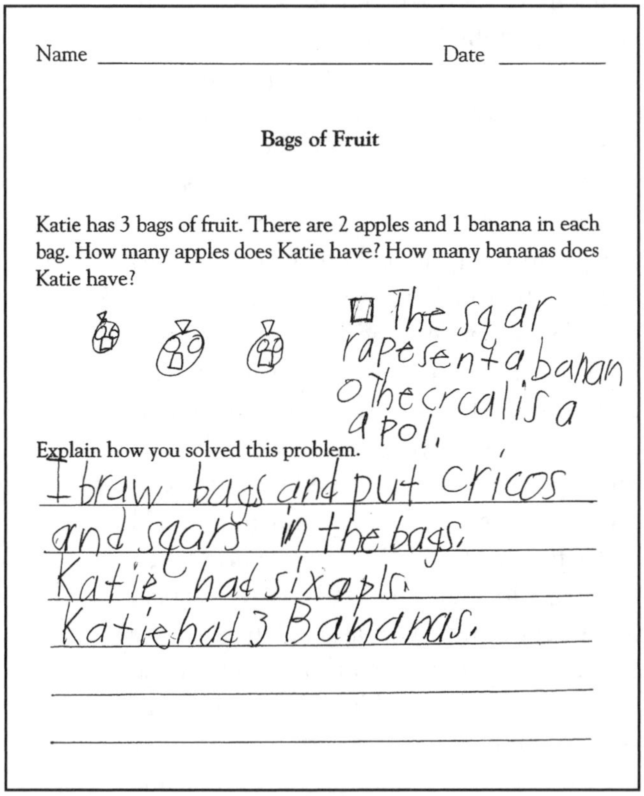
Name ______________________ Date __________

Bags of Fruit

Katie has 3 bags of fruit. There are 2 apples and 1 banana in each bag. How many apples does Katie have? How many bananas does Katie have?

☐ The sqar rapesent a banan
O The crcal is a apol.

Explain how you solved this problem.

I draw bags and put cricos and sqars in the bags.
Katie had sixapls.
Katie had 3 Bananas.

FIGURE 1.3 This first grader explains his work: "I draw bags and put circles and squares in the bags. Katie had 6 apples. Katie had 3 bananas." He includes a key showing that "the square represents a banana" and "the circle is an apple."

Use Logical Reasoning

Logical reasoning is a very abstract thinking skill. It requires students to organize clues or ideas and to draw conclusions based on them. Often students are given a seeming overload of confusing information and need to develop tools to organize the information so that it is in a useful form. Primary students might use 100 Charts (see Appendix C) to record and organize clues, while intermediate students might use logic matrix grids or Venn diagrams (see Appendix J) to sort more confusing information (O'Connell 2000). In this strategy, visualizing, organizing, and recording information helps students simplify the task. Discussions should focus on organizing data as well as identifying observation and inference skills that allow students to draw appropriate conclusions.

Work Backward

Working backward requires students to use inverse thinking as they explore problem situations. It provides a tool to solve problems in which the starting data is unknown, and it helps even primary students begin to develop key algebraic skills as they explore inverse operations by "undoing what was done." Students might be asked to determine how many pieces of candy Erica started with if she gave half to her friend, then gave 3 pieces to her brother, and had 2 pieces left for herself. By starting with what Erica had at the end of the problem, then working backward, students can determine the amount she had to begin with (see Figure 1.4). Using concrete materials to explore inverse thinking (e.g., using candy and undoing what was done, taking back candy that was given away) helps students visualize the thinking process.

Teaching problem-solving strategies is less about how to make the table or how to record the list and more about why making a table helps us see information more clearly or how making the list helps us keep thoughts

FIGURE 1.4 By using physical objects, this student was able to use inverse thinking as she reversed her actions to solve the problem.

organized. The strategy names are simple terms for students to remember and to use in discussions, but the ideas that lie beneath the terms are more complex and require discussion and reflection as teachers guide students to an understanding of the strategies. The ability to talk about strategies helps students share their thinking during problem-solving discussions. While they can be introduced in primary grades in quite simple forms, students can be continually challenged to explore the strategies in increasing complexity. For examples of strategy problems with various levels of complexity, see Appendix A.

How Can Teachers Help Students Understand the Problem-Solving Process?

Students gather, refine, and demonstrate mathematical ideas in a variety of ways. Some are abstract and intuitive learners who can do math in their heads, others are visual learners who benefit from seeing ideas, and still others gain from hands-on experiences in order to process ideas and apply information. Explorations, demonstrations, and discussions about problem-solving strategies provide the various students in the classroom with opportunities to see, hear, and do problem solving in a way that makes sense to them and in a way they can understand.

Problem solving is a multistep process and most textbooks and curricula support students in identifying how to work through the steps by providing a checklist or problem-solving process. Students move from (1) understanding the problem to (2) planning a way to get to a solution to (3) trying the plan to (4) checking the reasonableness of the answer to (5) reflecting on the solution and methods (O'Connell 2000). Helping students recognize the steps in their thinking as they solve problems is important, with verbal and written reflection being a key factor in the teaching of problem solving.

Assigning problems is not teaching problem solving. Teaching students to solve problems involves the use of a variety of instructional tools to support all of them in building their skills. It involves student explorations, small-group and whole-class discussions, and modeling and think-alouds by teachers. Strategies can be taught in ways that focus on student discourse, the development of thinking, and the uniqueness of solutions. It is not about students solving a problem with the strategy we had in mind; it is about them solving a problem with a strategy that makes sense and gets them to a solution.

Teacher demonstrations and modeling provide opportunities for students to hear and see strategies in use. Through think-aloud techniques teachers can share their ideas as they demonstrate solving a problem. Teachers share both content information (e.g., "One combination is a turkey sandwich and milk.") and process information (e.g., "I'm getting confused here. I think I better start over and get a plan so that I don't get confused.") during think-alouds. It is important for students to hear that others, even their teachers, feel confusion at times; however, after verbalizing that confusion, the next teacher comment should demonstrate that feelings of confusion should lead to reflections on ways to continue through the problem and ways to alleviate the confusion. The use of visuals during demonstrations (e.g., teacher uses physical models to show combinations, or records on the board as he talks about his combinations) helps students both see and hear the thinking process. For students who have not come up with ideas on their own, demonstrations help. For others, their ideas expand as they see different ways in which to solve problems.

It is critical to provide sufficient opportunities for student exploration when developing problem-solving strategies. The use of manipulatives allows students to have concrete and visual experiences as they solve problems. Manipulatives are used in mathematics when concepts are being developed and when we want students to *see* those concepts so that they can understand them better; manipulatives make invisible thinking skills

visible. In problem solving, ideas are often abstract, so seeing ideas in concrete ways can be enough to simplify problems. Getting ideas *out of* students' heads, into a format they can see and touch, helps them more easily comprehend what is being asked and allows them to explore solutions in concrete ways. For some manipulatives' templates, see Appendix C.

The use of calculators during problem-solving activities supports students by assisting them with computations and freeing them to focus on thinking skills. Calculators also allow students to explore the engaging data of real problems, data that may be beyond their computational skills. Allowing calculator use supports students in understanding and identifying technology tools that enhance their mathematical ability.

Traditionally, we view homework as a way of providing practice. By reviewing homework, teachers are able to determine if students can independently perform a task or apply a skill. In problem solving, however, homework can also be a tool to motivate and engage students; problems might be posed that will excite students and draw them into future classroom investigations. Homework provides opportunities for exploration and questioning because students can ponder problems at home and bring their insights to class for the next day's activity. The provision of various opportunities and frequent problem-solving practice through homework, centers, warm-ups, and class activities will strengthen students' abilities to apply the strategies to a variety of situations.

Group and partner work is critical to the acquisition of problem-solving skills. Through group work, students can share ideas and test their thinking on others. They are able to hear other ideas about solving problems, then fold those ideas into their own to further develop their thinking. Students often recognize misunderstandings when discussing their ideas and can then clarify or redirect their thinking. Limited ability students can be jump-started by group discussions, and those with higher levels of ability can solidify their ideas through the process of reviewing or explaining them to peers.

Facilitating discussions and debriefings following problem-solving tasks provides the ideal opportunity to extend thinking about mathematical concepts, as well as problem-solving approaches. According to the NCTM (2000, 55): "As teachers maintain an environment in which the development of understanding is consistently monitored through reflection, students are more likely to learn to take responsibility for reflecting on their work and make adjustments necessary when solving problems." Teachers may want to use a Thinking Chair to allow chosen students to present and discuss their thinking process and solution to others, or use Circle Time during which students gather in a circle to share their solutions as the teacher records ideas on a board or chart.

What Is the Teacher's Role During Problem-Solving Instruction?

Prior to problem-solving tasks, it is the teachers' responsibility to select meaningful activities to motivate students to *want to* find an answer. Such activities should explore meaningful math concepts. Teachers will need to decide whether manipulative use would be beneficial for students and whether the activity should be done in pairs, groups, or individually. The problem situation should be set up with a discussion and directions for completing the task. Discussing and/or conducting a demonstration of similar problems may generate ideas for ways to explore and to solve a problem.

During problem-solving activities, teachers need to provide support to students (see Figure 1.5). The teacher can prompt groups with questions or join discussions and gently

FIGURE 1.5　This teacher allows students to explain their thinking and supports them as they work toward a solution.

guide them, all the while listening to students and assessing their progress.

After problem-solving tasks are completed, teachers might conduct class debriefings to share the various methods for solving problems. Students might be asked to write about how they solved the problem or why they believe their answers are correct. Students might be asked to record the solutions and methods in their journals or to share their methods with a partner.

Throughout problem-solving lessons, the teacher is challenged to create a positive climate for solving problems within the classroom. The way in which teachers conduct class discussions or facilitate group activities helps to create a climate in which students are willing to take risks and share their thinking, cooperate with others within their group, persevere even when tasks are lengthy, and show respect for others' thinking. Patience, persistence, risk-taking, and cooperation are key attitudes crucial to problem-solving success (O'Connell 2000).

You can begin developing these skills within the classroom by praising students who demonstrate these qualities; for example: "I like the way Brendan and Brad shared ideas and worked together to figure out another way to approach that problem." "I'm glad to see that you hung in there and tried a few ways to get to the answer." Share situations when you needed those attitudes; for example, "I was ready to give up but then I remembered how good I felt when I finally solved the pizza problem, so I kept trying." Show students what is important; for example, "Your strategy didn't work, did it? But what a great idea to try."

When you sense that frustration is building in a student, step in to assist and redirect him or pair him with a partner who can help. If you sense that frustration is building in the whole class, take a time-out to discuss what is going on, redirect students' thoughts, and praise them for their efforts.

Both teachers and students have to learn to deal with moments of confusion during the problem-solving process. Students need to know that confusion is part of the learning process. Teachers need to be willing to witness student confusion as they struggle to find solutions. As understanding is built, everyone may get confused along the way. Mistakes are all okay; in fact, they often lead to discoveries.

How Can Teachers Meet the Needs of Students' Various Skill Levels During Problem-Solving Instruction?

Many students struggle with problem solving, but we can help them in a variety of ways. Using visual demonstrations and hands-on explorations will help those who need to see and to manipulate the problem situation. Working with a partner is a great support to struggling students or students with little confidence in their abilities. Using a think-aloud technique provides a model for effectively thinking about problem situations. Letting students use a calculator will relieve the pressure for those who have difficulty with calculation skills and allow them to focus on the thinking skills. Providing additional time or assigning fewer problems are modifications that may be needed by some students, and adapting the problem to make it simpler for students may be appropriate at times. Some students may need to begin a problem with a partner or as a whole group, but then are able to finish on their own. Icons in the classroom remind students of possible strategies (see Figure 1.6). Students often need a variety of supports as they attempt to make sense of math problems.

Many students are able to advance quickly in their problem-solving skills. It is important to continue to challenge these students with problems that require more sophisticated thinking. As the class explores strategies, consider posing more challenging versions of the problem to students with a high level of ability. Can you complicate the problem with a more complex pattern? Can you have students construct tables with three or four rows or with

FIGURE 1.6 Posted icons are visual reminders of the various strategies that might be used to solve problems.

students to apply several strategies to find the solution. Can you pose problems for which students need both to make a table and to do calculations based on data in that table? Moving toward more sophisticated problems will provide challenges for even the most capable students.

In addition, open-ended investigations (e.g., writing a proposal for a school fundraiser, deciding how to estimate the number of words on a page, figuring out how many hours of television they've watched) provide high achievers with opportunities to reason, plan, and justify. Don't forget to enlist students in the writing of problems of their own. Keep in mind, however, that although some students are able to find an answer quickly, they may still be unable to communicate how and why they solved the problem in the way they did. Modeling, think-alouds, and group work will help these students find the words to describe what happened in their heads as they moved toward a solution. Even students who can come up with answers quickly may need more time to develop the thinking that lies behind those answers.

more complicated data (e.g., fractions, decimals, percents)? Although we often begin by focusing on individual strategies so that students will recognize certain types of thinking (e.g., draw a picture, find a pattern, make a table), more sophisticated problems require

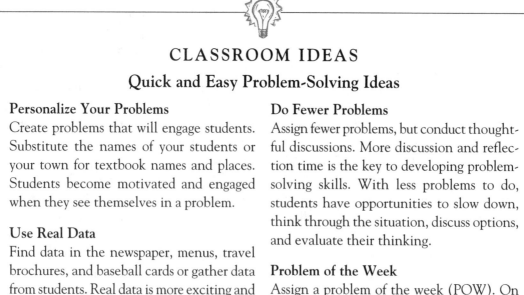

CLASSROOM IDEAS
Quick and Easy Problem-Solving Ideas

Personalize Your Problems
Create problems that will engage students. Substitute the names of your students or your town for textbook names and places. Students become motivated and engaged when they see themselves in a problem.

Use Real Data
Find data in the newspaper, menus, travel brochures, and baseball cards or gather data from students. Real data is more exciting and helps students see the meaningfulness of the math they are learning.

Do Fewer Problems
Assign fewer problems, but conduct thoughtful discussions. More discussion and reflection time is the key to developing problem-solving skills. With less problems to do, students have opportunities to slow down, think through the situation, discuss options, and evaluate their thinking.

Problem of the Week
Assign a problem of the week (POW). On Monday, review the problem and discuss any necessary directions. Throughout the week,

CLASSROOM IDEAS (continued)
Quick and Easy Problem-Solving Ideas

students can work on the problem as they have time, perhaps after they complete a class assignment, or for homework. On Friday, the class engages in a discussion of the POW with students sharing various methods. You might chart the different ways that students solved the problem on an overhead projector or a board.

Problem-Solving Bulletin Board
Designate a classroom bulletin board for problem solving. Post icons to remind students of possible strategies (O'Connell 2000). Display a problem, maybe a past POW, and a variety of student work samples to show different ways of solving the problem.

Read-Talk-Solve
Pair students so that they can begin problem-solving activities with the support of a partner. Ask students to read the problem together. Have them talk with their partners about how it might be solved. Students can then solve the problem together or individually.

Summary

Blending problem-centered instruction and the teaching of problem-solving strategies provides students with practice solving problems as well as opportunities to identify the ways in which they solve problems. As students explore math in problem contexts and focus on the development of critical thinking skills that assist them in proceeding toward a solution, they become better and more confident problem solvers.

On the CD-ROM

Appendix A—Sample Strategy Problems
Appendix C—Manipulative Templates

Suggested Resources

Carpenter, Thomas P., Elizabeth Fennema, Megan Loef Franke, Linda Levi, and Susan B. Empson. 1999. *Children's Mathematics: Cognitively Guided Instruction*. Portsmouth, NH: Heinemann.

Questions for Reflection

1. Were you taught how to solve math problems or were you assigned problems to solve? How might a focus on strategies have helped you develop and refine your skills?
2. Can all students become math problem solvers? What instructional strategies will help them?
3. Look at some student work. Analyze the various ways students solve problems. Is there one correct way? Is there a more efficient way?
4. In what ways can you continue to challenge intuitive problem solvers within your classroom?
5. In what ways can you help struggling problem solvers feel more confident and increase their problem-solving skills?

Lester, Frank K., and Randall I. Charles, eds. 2003. *Teaching Mathematics Through Problem Solving: Prekindergarten–Grade 6*. Reston, VA: National Council of Teachers of Mathematics.

O'Connell, Susan R. 2000. *Introduction to Problem Solving: Strategies for the Elementary Math Classroom*. Portsmouth, NH: Heinemann.

Sakshaug, Lynae E., Melfried Olson, and Judith Olson. 2002. *Children Are Mathematical Problem Solvers*. Reston, VA: National Council of Teachers of Mathematics.

Whitin, David J., and Robin Cox. 2003. *A Mathematical Passage: Strategies for Promoting Inquiry in Grades 4–6*. Portsmouth, NH: Heinemann.

Staff Development Training Videos

Increasing Students' Math Problem-Solving Skills—Part I: Developing Core Problem-Solving Strategies, Grades 3–6. 2004. Bellevue, WA: Bureau of Education and Research.

Increasing Students' Math Problem-Solving Skills—Part II: Expanding Students' Repertoire of Problem-Solving Strategies, Grades 3–6. 2004. Bellevue, WA: Bureau of Education and Research.

CHAPTER TWO

Helping Students Understand Basic Facts and Computations

Traditionally, learning computations was a matter of memorizing basic facts and computational procedures. Teachers demonstrated algorithms and then students practiced until they were able to repeat the procedures. While students who possessed strong memory skills and an ability to bring their own understanding to computations faired well with those techniques, many others were unable to master mathematics simply by memorizing a series of rote skills and procedures.

Students must know basic facts and how to compute fluently, but they should also understand basic operations and computations. The National Council of Teachers of Mathematics (NCTM) affirms that "understanding numbers and operations, developing number sense, and gaining fluency in arithmetic computation form the core of mathematics education for the elementary grades" (2000, 32). This chapter explores instructional strategies that support students' understanding and retention of computational skills.

Why Is It So Important to Understand Basic Facts and Algorithms?

Each skill or concept students learn builds on their prior knowledge. At the core of students' math understandings are basic computational understandings. Without knowledge of basic computations, how can students explore concepts related to fractions or decimals or apply ideas to money, measurement, or geometry? At the core of understanding mathematics are the basics of numbers and operations. A strong foundation allows students to connect new knowledge and build more complex mathematical understandings.

While knowing facts and procedures is an important skill, it is the ability to apply knowledge that is most useful to students. It is the ability to use facts to solve problems that is the optimal goal; recall alone is only for classroom exercises. To apply and retain computational skills, there must be a high level of understanding of them (Fennema and

Romberg 1999). Before students practice and memorize, they should understand the ideas behind procedures. "Developing fluency requires a balance and connection between conceptual understanding and computational proficiency" (NCTM 2000, 35).

Students who merely memorize facts and procedures without understanding may quickly forget them; they will have no way to find an answer if facts and procedures are forgotten. Corwin contends that "children may learn arithmetic procedures by repetition alone; if so, their only tool for recalling how to find solutions is their memory. Mathematics, rather than resting on a rich base of exploration, discovery, conversation, and common sense, may rest exclusively on the relatively weak platform of memory" (1996, 2). Students who engage in conceptual discussions and investigations in which they explore and invent meaningful computational strategies are building a strong foundation for necessary future mathematical skills.

What Are Invented Procedures and How Are They Helpful?

In the past, teachers simply showed students how to do traditional algorithms; however, in today's math classrooms, we see evidence of students building strong understandings of numbers and operations through activities that allow them to invent procedures that make sense to them. Rather than memorizing a series of rules, procedures, or formulas, students make sense of the math in the problem and figure out ways to find solutions. Discussions about students' methods allow them to share their thinking, refine their ideas, and test their procedures to see if they work in all situations. Through these investigations and discussions, students invent algorithms that *make sense* to them. A strong computational foundation can result from activities in which students learn computations through invented procedures and classroom discussions, as well as standard algorithms (NCTM 2000).

A group of second graders explored a problem about seating arrangements for a pizza party. They were asked to determine how many people could be at the party if there were 4 square tables with a person seated on each side of every table. Students shared their ideas in the following ways.

- Aidan—"I did 4 + 4 + 4 + 4 and got 16 people because I knew there would be 4 people and I had to add them 4 times for all of the tables."

- Caroline—"I did 4 + 4 and got 8, then I did another 8 and got 16."

These two students demonstrated an understanding of the problem as well as reasonable strategies for finding the solution. Caroline found a partial sum and recognized that she could just double it to find the total. Although the procedures were different, both worked effectively to find the solution.

Some third graders explored a problem in which they were asked to determine the number of children at a ball game with 46 girls and 34 boys. Grace determined that there were 80 children at the game and explained her computational method: "I took 40 + 30 and got 70, then I took 6 + 4 and got 10; so 70 + 10 is 80." While Grace did not do the addition problem using the standard algorithm, her method makes sense and would work with other numbers. In fact, when asked to add two-digit numbers, many people would use a method similar to Grace's because they find it easier than the traditional algorithm they were taught.

As students are given opportunities to invent procedures to solve problems, they explore numbers, discuss ideas, and often recognize other ways to do them. Through teacher-facilitated discussions, students examine their ideas and further develop their concepts about numbers and operations. They ponder whether their method will always work or whether another students' method might be easier or more efficient. In traditional algorithms, we often ask students to memorize procedures that make no sense to them. They memorize words about placeholders or trading or carrying or cross-multiplying, but the words are not connected to a real understanding of numbers. Allowing students to explore problems and invent procedures will help them build understanding; it promotes reasoning rather than memorizing.

Students do benefit from learning traditional algorithms—as one way to achieve computational fluency—as well as from being allowed to invent different procedures. While students may begin by solving problems in nonroutine ways to make sense of math processes, the teacher can use students' ideas as a starting point for examining traditional methods. As students explore math through problem situations and focus on understanding math processes, they are building number sense, developing problem-solving skills, and arriving at a better understanding of computational procedures.

How Can Teachers Support Students' Understanding of Numbers and Operations?

The foundation for understanding numbers and operations begins in primary classrooms with the concept of counting. Rather than just saying and writing numbers, students need to understand those numbers. Having students explore four objects in a variety of ways helps them understand the concept of "four." Having them compare four objects to groups with more or less objects, or line up objects to determine one-to-one correspondence, contributes to their understanding of numbers. Older students continue to develop their number sense as they explore connections between numbers through discussions of more than, less than, same as, twice as much, three times more, and so on.

Exploring patterns greatly supports students' understanding of numbers and operations. Skip-counting helps students recognize and understand patterns and helps strengthen their number sense. As students practice a variety of ways to skip-count (e.g., by 2s, 3s, 4s, 5s, 10s, etc.), they familiarize themselves with the patterns in our number system. Teachers can help make them visible to students by using 100 Charts or number lines (see Appendix C) to show the patterns as students skip-count.

Many teachers capitalize on opening-of-the-day calendar activities to explore numbers and patterns. By placing calendar dates on circles, squares, or triangles, students can explore patterns throughout the month; or by discussing yesterday's date, what the date is in three days or next Tuesday, students begin to recognize patterns and strengthen their understanding of numbers. While such activities are more prevalent in primary-grade classrooms, many intermediate teachers are modifying the technique to use calendars to highlight multiples or more intricate patterns.

It is important that students first understand the mathematics before they are asked to memorize facts and procedures (Burns 1992a, Van de Walle 2004). Beginning basic computational lessons with problem situations helps set a context for the computations and allows students to hear scenarios to illustrate the operations. Reading children's literature that illustrates various operations sets a context for learning and understanding those operations. Connecting facts and procedures to real-world activities gives students a real context in which to understand math. Students might add the number of runs in each inning to find a baseball score, or subtract the cost of admission to the zoo from the money in their pockets, or multiply the cost of lunch by the number of students ordering lunch today, or divide the pieces in the manipulative bucket between the students in a group to determine how many pieces each person will receive.

Mental math activities help students develop number sense and provide practice in applying basic skills. While waiting in line for lunch, students might be asked to mentally compute sums or products. Teachers might verbally pose computation chains for students to solve (e.g., $3 \times 5 + 2 - 1$) to stimulate their mental math skills. Teachers might pose story problems for students to mentally compute. Estimation activities provide opportunities for students to demonstrate their understanding of mathematics, as well as opportunities for teachers to help modify those understandings through discussions about how they arrived at the estimates.

How Can Teachers Help Students Develop Strategies to Understand and Retain Basic Facts?

Students who use strategies combined with memorization will have a better foundation for understanding and retaining math facts. Prior to memorization, students need to explore problem situations to experience the operations, as well as see visual models to help them more fully understand each operation. Students should be encouraged to discuss the operations and explore strategies to help them understand the process and figure out an answer.

To understand the concept of addition, students should be supported as they explore the concept of joining two sets. A common strategy for finding answers to addition problems is counting on (e.g., the answer to $5 + 2$ can be determined by counting on to 5 by saying 5, 6, 7). Students should also be supported in seeing turn-around numbers—the commutative property—through many examples to illustrate that $4 + 2$ will be the same as $2 + 4$. Still another way that students find addition answers is through using what they already know to figure out unknown equations. Beginning with doubles (e.g., $2 + 2$, $3 + 3$, etc.) gives students a foundation so that they can figure out other sums based on their knowledge of doubles. If $2 + 2 = 4$, then $2 + 3$ must be 4 plus 1 more. Helping students use facts they know to find answers to unknown facts provides them with a useful strategy that can be applied to other operations.

The concept of subtraction can be viewed in several ways. The idea of *take away* is one way to view subtraction, but subtraction is also the operation used when items are compared (e.g., Kate had 6 pieces of bubble gum. Jason had 8 pieces of bubble gum. Who had more bubble gum?). Lining up objects to show the act of comparing will help students see this subtraction concept as they formulate $8 - 6 = 2$ to find the difference between the two rows of objects (see Figure 2.1).

Another model for subtraction is the missing addend model. Often, we use the phrase "how many more" to illustrate this way of viewing subtraction. For example, Brendan had 4 tickets for the rides. He needed 7 tickets to ride the roller coaster. How many more tickets did he need? You can think of this problem as $7 - 4$, but often it is thought of as $4 + ? = 7$ (i.e., 4 plus how many more will give me 7). Discussions about similar problems will help students see this type of problem with more clarity. The various models of subtraction should be reviewed through manipulative activities and story problems, or explored through literature, so that students develop an

FIGURE 2.1 This primary student uses linking cubes to compare groups of objects as she explores subtraction concepts.

understanding of the concept of subtraction. When helping students explore strategies for finding answers to subtraction problems, it is helpful to relate subtraction to addition through fact-family explorations.

The concept of multiplication can be illustrated through manipulative demonstrations or student explorations that show the joining of equal sets. Arrays and area grids, such as those in Figures 2.2 and 2.3, also illustrate the concept of multiplication. In exploring multiplication strategies, students often equate it with the idea of repeated addition. To help them conceptualize multiplication facts, students can be asked to connect facts to real situations. Direct students to look at the 5 fingers on their hands—how many fingers are on 2 hands? Or 5 might be viewed as how many cents there are in a nickel, so how many cents are in 3 nickels? Three might

be seen as the wheels on a tricycle—how many wheels are on 2 tricycles?

As students begin to struggle to memorize multiplication facts, it is important to facilitate discussions about strategies for finding an answer prior to asking them to memorize. Encourage students to start with facts they know and to build from there. In multiplication, students discover that multiplying by two is like doubling. Once they know the two times tables, they recognize that fours are just the twos doubled. Students recognize the fives by thinking about familiar counting sequences (e.g., skip-counting). If they know doubles (e.g., $6 \times 6 = 36$), then 7×6 is 1 more 6, so it is 42. Or some students might break down 6×5 as a set of 2×5 and 2×5 and 2×5. Through these insights, students are exploring the concept of multiplication as they are developing valid strategies to find solutions.

Understanding division requires understanding the concepts of repeated subtraction and fair sharing. Again, the use of stories or manipulatives helps students see repeated subtraction. For example, Allison has a bag of 21 pieces of candy; she gives one child 7 pieces, another child 7 pieces, another child 7 pieces, and is then out of candy. She has subtracted 7 from her bag of candy 3 different times. Or think about Pat who shares a tray of 12 cookies with 3 friends; this helps students explore the fair-sharing model. As he sorts the cookies into fair (equal) groups, he is illustrating the concept of division. Students can be asked how many sets of cookies will be created or how many cookies will be in each set. Memorizing division facts may be unnecessary because students generally view division as a missing factor equation. Helping students see that 12 divided by 4 is the same as $4 \times ? = 12$ gets them to use the multiplication facts they know to solve division problems.

Keep in mind that discussions about basic operations should not be limited to the primary grades. As numbers become more complex and students are challenged with problems that require computations with fractions, decimals, percents, or large numbers,

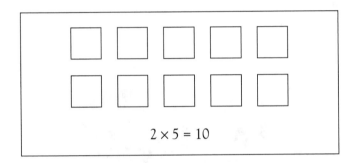

$2 \times 5 = 10$

FIGURE 2.2   Students can create arrays—arrangements of objects in rows and columns—to visualize the multiplication concept.

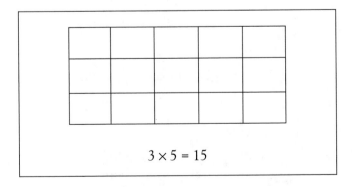

$3 \times 5 = 15$

FIGURE 2.3   Students can show multiplication facts by creating area grids on graph paper.

they will benefit from discussions about problem scenarios and reflections on the concepts of the operations. The sight of fractions or decimals often causes anxiety that can block students from seeing the problem situation. Replacing more complex numbers with simpler ones, and discussing the scenario using the simpler numbers, generally helps students identify the operation that is reflected in the problem situation. Discussing the concepts behind basic operations should be a routine activity at all elementary grade levels.

Should Students Be Asked to Memorize Basic Facts?

Memorization of math facts is necessary to facilitate mental math, to provide students with fluency during computations, and to move easily through problem situations. But, memorizing numbers and symbols without a basic understanding can be very difficult for many students. There are a variety of ways to reinforce and practice facts; however, practice and memorization should occur after students have explored the concepts for the operations.

While many textbooks and curricula push students to master basic facts in a chapter approach (e.g., a unit on basic multiplication facts that asks students to master all facts over several weeks' time), there is tremendous value in repeated practice over extended periods of time. Students need continued practice to commit basic facts to memory, regardless of the grade level. Rather than lengthy drills, many teachers have seen the benefits of short, engaging practice sessions spanning the school year. Flash cards are a tried-and-true practice activity, but there are many other activities that engage students in the practice of basic facts, from card games to bingo to memory games to sorting activities (see Figure 2.4). At all grade levels, fun and engaging fact practice provides support to students so that retention of facts is possible. For some fun math fact activities to help students review and retain basic facts, see Appendix B.

FIGURE 2.4 Students practice basic facts using math scopes, a variation of standard flash cards.

The National Council of Teachers of Mathematics (2000) supports the use of calculators, particularly in problem-solving situations; they help students solve problems that may be beyond their current computational skills. Calculators also help students explore math operations as they investigate patterns and operations by looking at and discussing the results generated by them. The NCTM views the calculator as a tool for problem solving or computational explorations, but recognizes that for basic facts practice, their use may not be appropriate (2000). The choice of when to allow use of calculators in the classroom is an instructional decision based on your math objectives for the lesson. If the purpose of the lesson is to provide students with practice in computations, then the use of a calculator would not support your goal.

How Can Teachers Assess Students' Understanding of Numbers and Operations?

Assessing students' understanding of numbers and operations goes deeper than checking for correct answers. While answers always provide some information about student understanding, our goal is to determine if students have developed number sense as well as an understanding of operations and computational procedures. Various assessment techniques will provide that information. Observations of student work and attention to their comments inform us about their level of understanding. Informal student interviews (e.g., a series of questions probing their ideas) also can be an invaluable tool. Tasks in which students are asked to draw pictures or write stories to illustrate equations offer insight into their understandings. Having students write an explanation of how they did a procedure (e.g., adding fractions with unlike denominators) helps us see their thinking as they describe how they approached the task. For some ideas about writing descriptions of math tasks, see Appendix H.

Although tests of math facts are used frequently to assess students' mastery of the basics, timed ones are discouraged because they contribute to students' anxiety and often undermine their motivation to learn facts. Rather than students competing with each other, many teachers have students chart their own progress (e.g., facts known sheets); they can keep track of their individual achievements and develop pride in their own growth.

CLASSROOM IDEAS
Quick and Easy Computation Activities

Do Not "Learn 'em and Leave 'em."
Try not to move too rapidly through initial attempts at memorizing math facts. Even if students appear to know the facts during the "multiplication unit," they will forget them without continued practice. Make facts practice a part of the daily routine through warm-up and closure activities, centers (see Appendix K), or partner reviews. Even activities as simple as frequent two-minute flash card reviews will help students maintain skills.

Pinch Cards
Pinch cards are an all-pupil response technique in which each student is given an index card that displays grade-level appropriate operation signs. Second graders might have pinch cards that display addition and subtraction signs, while fourth or fifth graders

CLASSROOM IDEAS (continued)
Quick and Easy Computation Activities

might have pinch cards displaying all four operations. The teacher poses a word problem and students pinch the part of the card that indicates the operation that should be used to solve the problem (see Figure 2.5). This activity provides students with practice listening to and analyzing problem situations to determine the related operation, affords an opportunity for informal discussions about operations, and provides teachers with a quick check on students' understanding (O'Connell 2000).

Triangle Flash Cards

Working on the missing-factor multiplication model may be more useful to students than drilling division facts because that is how most of us view division problems. With triangle flash cards, the factors and product are placed on the three corners of the card (see Appendix B). The factors are written in blue and the product in red. The teacher, or student partner, covers one number and the student has to find the product or missing factor. Triangle flash cards provide practice

with multiplication and division facts and help students see division as missing-factor multiplication.

Variation: Create triangle flash cards to review addition and subtraction. Addends should be written in blue and the sum in red. As one number is covered, the student needs to add to find the sum (if the numbers are both blue) or subtract to find the missing addend (subtract the blue from the red).

Less Is More

Modify the quantity of calculations by cutting the paper in half, crossing off every other problem, or circling only the problems students are to complete. Do fewer computations with more talk about those computations. Rather than just doing them, discuss the how and why of the computations.

What's the Question?

Provide students with an answer and ask them to come up with a possible equation that would result in that answer. If the answer is 25, students can generate equations such as the following: $10 + 15 = 25$, $5 \times 5 = 25$, $100 - 75 = 25$, $24 + 1 = 25$. For older students, use more complex numbers such as $4\frac{1}{2}$ or 1.45.

Variation: Students can be asked to write story problems that would result in that answer. Answers might include 25%, 4 pounds, 16 feet, or $2\frac{1}{2}$ candy bars. Students should be challenged to justify that the answers make sense for the problems they have created.

Chunking Practice Sessions

When working on computational skills (e.g., adding two-digit numbers, multiplying fractions), consider an alternative to traditional teacher-directed lessons followed by lengthy

FIGURE 2.5   As the teacher poses a problem, this student uses a pinch card to indicate the operation she believes will solve the problem.

CLASSROOM IDEAS (continued)
Quick and Easy Computation Activities

practice sessions by chunking the practice into shorter sessions. Rather than a single demonstration followed by extended practice, consider a demonstration followed by a short practice session (maybe three problems). Walk through the room and observe students at work. Use what's observed to then demonstrate the procedure again, talking through your actions. Engage students in discussions to verify their understanding. Then assign two to three problems for student practice and rotate through the room to observe them again. This modified whole-class approach will provide shorter practice sessions that will hold their interest, and it allows you to catch errors before students

have committed them to memory through lengthy practice sessions.

Quick Check
This cumulative review technique helps students review and retain previously taught skills. Designate a day of the week (e.g., Tuesday Review) so that it is a regular part of the math routine. Three to five varied computations are posed. Students complete the short activities, then the solutions are reviewed aloud with the class. The teacher uses think-aloud techniques to talk through the solutions or asks students to talk through the solutions.

Summary

Students need to know basic facts. They need to be able to perform math computations fluently to arrive at answers to even simple mathematics tasks. Both invented procedures and standard algorithms have a place in the classroom. By learning computations through models, discussions, problem scenarios, demonstrations, and investigations, students are better able to understand, retain, and apply facts and procedures to real situations and/or more complex math tasks.

 On the CD-ROM

Appendix B—Activities to Review Basic Math Facts and Computation Skills
Appendix C—Manipulative Templates
Appendix H—Math Writing Tasks
Appendix K—Math Centers

Suggested Resources

Carpenter, Thomas P., Elizabeth Fennema, Megan Loef Franke, Linda Levi, and Susan B. Empson. 1999. *Children's Mathematics: Cognitively Guided Instruction.* Portsmouth, NH: Heinemann.

Questions for Reflection

1. How do invented procedures support students' understanding of numbers and operations?
2. In what ways can teachers provide repeated, but engaging, practice with basic facts?
3. What is the purpose of timed math fact tests? What are the drawbacks? In what ways can facts be reviewed without those drawbacks?
4. In what ways can you support students who struggle with memorizing basic math facts?

Miller, Marcia, and Martin Lee. 1997. *The Mega-Fun Multiplication Facts Activity Book*. New York: Scholastic.

O'Connell, Susan R. 2000. *Introduction to Problem Solving: Strategies for the Elementary Math Classroom*. Portsmouth, NH: Heinemann.

Sharp, Janet M., and Karen Bush Hoiberg. 2005. *Learning and Teaching K–8 Mathematics*. Boston: Pearson Education.

Van de Walle, John A. 2004. *Elementary and Middle School Mathematics—Teaching Developmentally*. Boston: Pearson Education.

CHAPTER THREE

Developing Math Concepts Through Manipulatives

A look into today's mathematics classrooms reveals students touching, moving, and talking about math in a concrete way thanks to the widespread use of manipulatives. Rather than learning mathematics as abstract ideas, manipulatives bring it to life for students and allow them to construct math understanding. This chapter discusses the use of manipulatives as a teacher tool to demonstrate math skills and concepts, as well as a tool for students to use as they actively solve problems and investigate ideas. For both purposes, manipulatives have become a critical component of elementary math instruction.

Why Use Manipulatives in the Math Classroom?

Manipulatives enhance the teaching of mathematics at all grade levels. The use of manipulatives in the math classroom allows students to see concrete examples of abstract ideas (Burns 2002). Students can see that 6 is more than 2, experience the process of subtracting two-digit numbers, and discover the meaning of equivalent fractions. Instead of talking about abstract ideas, students can touch and see and move objects to explore, and ulti-

mately to make sense of, mathematical ideas. Rowan and Bourne describe manipulatives as "props with which children explore mathematics concepts" (2001, 81).

Manipulatives engage and motivate students; when introduced during lessons, kids get excited! As teachers pass out geoboards, multilink blocks, or tangrams (see Appendix C), students get interested in what is coming next. Manipulatives make them curious and involve them in active learning rather than listening and observing; they are moving chips, creating figures, or physically comparing quantities. With manipulatives, teaching and learning become student-centered as students build their own understanding through experiences instead of being told to memorize procedures and formulas.

Manipulatives help students visualize and communicate about math ideas. As students see concepts, they can test understandings, record observations, and talk about insights. Students are able to visualize and discuss patterns using 100 Charts and chips (see Appendix C). They can see and talk about subtraction and "how many more" as two sets of cubes are lined up and compared. Manipulatives give students something to talk about and reflect on (Van de Walle 2004).

Manipulatives provide students with an important tool for solving problems as they learn to represent and organize ideas visually. Using Venn diagrams (see Appendix J) to sort buttons by attributes (i.e. size, color, number of holes) allows even young students to categorize them based on similarities and differences. Intermediate students might use square tiles to explore problems about area and perimeter (see Figure 3.1). As students engage in problem-solving tasks, manipulatives help them visualize problem conditions and effectively move toward solutions.

Students remember what they experience. We have all heard the old Chinese proverb, "Tell me and I'll forget; show me and I may remember; involve me and I'll understand." Do you remember the worksheets you did in elementary school? Probably not, but how many of us remember the hands-on experiences as we did an interesting science investigation or dug our hands into an art project. When experiences are committed to memory, those memories serve as anchors to which students can compare new ideas and experiences. Are students more likely to remember the chart in the text that lists items that weigh one pound or the hands-on investigation in which they weigh real objects and discover that their math book weighs one pound? The memory of that math book weighing one pound will serve as a benchmark for later experiences with weights. Manipulative activities are memorable!

Observing students work with manipulatives allows teachers to see what they know about a concept or skill. Their actions make their thinking visible. Aristotle said, "One must learn by doing the thing, for though you think you know it, you have no certainty until you try." Doing math with manipulatives forces students to get math out of their heads and helps them see whether they truly understand a concept. In addition, observing their actions helps us assess the level to which students understand math.

How Should Manipulatives Be Used?

Simply giving students manipulatives does not make a meaningful math task. Manipulatives are tools to enhance math teaching and learning, not activities in and of themselves. Meaningful math tasks have a purpose; they need to be linked to standards. Tasks should promote inquiry and thought and be relevant to students' abilities and interests, with a focus on understanding and application. While tangrams or attribute blocks or color tiles may engage them, simply presenting a manipulative activity with no connection to standards and no thought to lesson objectives will not expand students' understandings.

Traditionally, manipulatives have been used to enhance the teaching of numeration, measurement, and geometry skills. Figure 3.2 shows a primary student who was given cubes to explore measurement. Base-ten blocks are used to help students understand place value, addition, subtraction, or the decimal system. Using Cuisenaire rods helps students explore fractions and ratios, and geoboards, pattern blocks, and tangrams (see Appendix C) help students understand spatial concepts. But

FIGURE 3.1   This fourth grader uses square tiles to explore the concept of area.

FIGURE 3.2   This kindergarten student measures the length of her foot as she places blocks across her traced foot outline.

manipulatives are also great tools for enhancing reasoning and problem solving. While teachers might demonstrate the use of a certain manipulative to solve a problem, students should be able to choose the tool that makes sense to them. Having a variety of manipulatives available during problem-solving tasks allows students to access them as needed.

Manipulatives can be integrated into whole-class lessons, small-group activities, or individual explorations. Teachers might model decimal concepts for the class by using transparent base-ten blocks on an overhead projector. During small-group activities, students might explore probability with investigations using two-color counters, and individual students might be asked to explore volume with their own set of color cubes. A student center might challenge students to use fraction circles (see Appendix C) to discover equivalent fractions.

How Can Teachers Prepare for Effective Use of Manipulatives?

The use of manipulatives engages students in mathematical tasks and assists them in developing mathematical concepts; however, using manipulatives can pose a management problem for teachers. Advance preparation will help ensure a smooth and meaningful lesson and provide students with a structure to explore ideas in a guided way. Prior to deciding to use manipulatives, it might be helpful to consider the following questions.

- Will the manipulative help achieve my objective?
- Which manipulative will work best to develop the concept?
- Should students work alone? In pairs? In groups?
- Do I have the time to appropriately use manipulatives?
- Can this lesson be done using a demonstration with manipulatives on an overhead or is the objective best achieved through a hands-on experience?

If students have had no previous experience with manipulatives, you may want to allow them some time to explore prior to the actual math activity. In this way, students will have a chance to exercise their curiosity about the new manipulative so that they can focus on the actual task later. Teachers might place baskets of manipulatives at centers where students can explore them during morning routines or when classroom assignments are completed, or teachers might schedule a brief exploration time for all students prior to the task.

Initial experiences with manipulatives may be more directed as the teacher provides essential information on how a manipulative can be used and reviews key ideas to help students accurately engage in the activity (e.g., understanding base-ten blocks as the cube being one unit, the rod being one 10, the flat being one 100). Many teachers provide brief demonstrations using transparent manipulatives on an overhead projector before beginning the independent task.

Giving clear and specific directions before distributing manipulatives is a critical teacher responsibility. Explaining the task, informing students of time limitations, and clarifying expectations for behavior are critical preparatory activities. If necessary, written activity instructions can be included with student materials or recorded on chart paper or the board for students to refer to during the activity.

Preparation of materials prior to a manipulative task will help the activity begin more smoothly. Items should be assembled in quantities that work for the activity and should be ready to distribute. Teachers can use student helpers to distribute the precounted bags or baskets of materials. Prior to manipulative distribution, it is always good to anticipate any problems that could occur (e.g., rubber bands being shot during geoboard activities, toothpicks being used to poke other students). Students need to be fully aware of how to use manipulatives and what constitutes misuse of them, as well as the consequences for misuse. Students enjoy activities that involve manipulatives and most teachers find that simply revoking the privilege of using a manipulative for a class session will curb the negative behavior of students who are misusing them.

What Is the Teacher's Role During Manipulative Activities?

During a manipulative activity, it is the teacher's job to move around the room and observe and assist students. Teachers can prompt and guide students with questions and encourage them to record information or thoughts while they are working (e.g., making notes in learning logs). Teachers may need to support struggling students with questions, suggestions, or observations, or they may want to pose a second-tier assignment for students who work quickly and need to be challenged with a more complex level of the task.

Primary students may have difficulty making the connection between manipulative activities and abstract mathematics. They often do not see the connection between the cubes they use in class and the numbers on a worksheet. Teachers can help students bridge the gap from concrete to abstract by showing

representations as they work with manipulatives. As students see their experiences written in symbolic form, or discussed in more abstract ways, they begin to see the connection between their concrete experiences and the resulting abstract ideas or symbols.

Student behavior should be constantly monitored during manipulative activities. As teachers move throughout the classroom, gentle reminders of behavior expectations may be needed. Consequences for misbehavior should be consistent so that students recognize that manipulative use has rules that will be enforced.

What Is the Teacher's Role After Work Sessions with Manipulatives?

Closure is a critical lesson component. Students can be asked to record their insights and observations in a log or journal after working with manipulatives. Primary students can draw and label what was done, while intermediate students can be told to include written reflections about what was learned. Also, students can share their observations through partner or class discussions. If the manipulatives were used in a problem-solving activity, problems, strategies, and solutions should be discussed, as well as a discussion regarding which manipulatives were helpful in visualizing problems and finding solutions. Following each manipulative activity, students should be given an opportunity to share their insights and summarize their learning.

Many teachers record their own observations about student work following manipulative activities. It may be as simple as a check noting evidence of understanding and a minus noting evidence of confusion. Extension activities can then be developed and placed at classroom centers to either challenge advanced students or provide repeated exposure for struggling students. While some students may "graduate" from using manipulatives and begin to use more pictorial or abstract methods for solving problems, others may continue to need manipulatives. Having them available within the classroom for those students will be a great support.

Being able to quickly and efficiently collect materials and store them for future use can be a challenge. Providing specific directions for the return and storage of materials is critical. Having student helpers speeds up their collection, and having an organized storage system will pay big dividends when you choose to use the materials again.

Which Manipulatives Should Be Used for Elementary Math Instruction?

You will need to decide which manipulatives to include in lessons based on your objectives and budget. Some manipulatives can be used to illustrate multiple math concepts. Color tiles can be used in third grade to explore area and perimeter, to create models of multiplication as students build rectangles to show 3×4, or to study fractional concepts as students investigate $\frac{1}{2}$ or $\frac{3}{4}$ of a set of tiles. Commonly used manipulatives for the primary level include Unifix cubes, number lines, two-color counters, base-ten blocks, color tiles, multilink blocks, sorting objects, counters, clocks, balance scales, thermometers, measuring jars, cups and spoons, pattern blocks, rulers, fraction pieces, solid geometric models, geoboards, coins, and spinners, see Appendix C. At the intermediate level, it is common to see the following manipulatives in classrooms: two-color counters, base-ten blocks, color tiles, multilink blocks, rulers, fraction pieces, Cuisenaire rods, pattern blocks, geoboards, solid geometric models, tangrams, mirrors, coins, spinners, balance scale and weights, various capacity containers, measuring cups and spoons, thermometers, rulers, tape measures, compasses, and protractors.

Rather than purchasing commercial manipulatives, many teachers choose to use everyday objects as manipulatives or to create their own hand-made ones (see Figure 3.3). Macaroni, paper clips, or beans can be used as chips or counters. Squares cut from index cards or tag board can take the place of color tiles. Craft sticks and beans can replace base-ten blocks. Many geometric shapes can be created with toothpicks, and toothpicks connected by gumdrops or miniature marshmallows can be used to create three-dimensional figures. Real coins can be used for money activities. Students can create their own fraction kits using strips of construction paper that have been folded, cut, and labeled as different fractional parts (Burns 1992a). Sugar cubes can be used instead of wooden or plastic cubes. For templates to create a variety of paper or tag board manipulatives, see Appendix C. Don't forget the possibility of electronic manipulatives, either (see more about these in Chapter 10).

Math Topic	Commercial Manipulatives	Inexpensive or Teacher-Created Alternatives
Whole number operations	Colored chips Base-ten blocks Cuisenaire rods Unifix cubes	Toothpicks Macaroni Beans Craft sticks and beans
Time	Clocks	Hand-made clocks
Measurement	Scales Measuring cups and spoons Capacity containers of various sizes Cuisenaire rods Rulers Meter or yard sticks Trundle wheels Square tiles Cubes	Paper clips Kitchen measuring cups and spoons Sugar cubes
Geometry	Attribute blocks Geometric solids Pattern blocks Tangrams Square tiles Geoboards Multilink blocks Cubes Compasses Protractors	Hand-made Wikki sticks (yarn dipped in wax) Toothpicks Marshmallows or gum drops
Fractions	Fraction circles Fraction bars Colored chips Base-ten blocks Cuisenaire rods	Hand-made fraction strips Folded paper Colored paper squares
Decimals	Base-ten blocks	Paper strips and squares
Probability/data analysis	Two-colored counters Colored chips Spinners Dice Coins	Colored paper squares Colored candies Hand-made spinners
Reasoning/logic	Attribute blocks	Buttons/plastic sorting objects

FIGURE 3.3 Frequently used manipulatives

CLASSROOM IDEAS
Quick and Easy Ideas for Managing Manipulative Use

Be Prepared

Have all manipulative materials prepared in advance. Be sure to have enough for each child, pair, or group. Organize group baskets or plastic bags with all of the necessary supplies for the activity (e.g., for a group of 4, the basket should include 4 dice, 4 spinners, 4 worksheets, 4 calculators). Assign a student in each group to pick up the basket or bag for her group. This student will also be responsible for returning the materials to a central classroom location after the activity and may be asked to inventory materials to be sure all have been returned.

Have a Signal

Have a zero-noise signal (e.g., the flickering of classroom lights, a 5-4-3-2-1 countdown, or a clapping pattern) to quiet students temporarily in case whole-class discussions or further directions are needed. During this quiet time, all student explorations must stop. It is a "no noise" and "hands-off" signal. With primary students, it may be necessary to ask them to place manipulatives in the corner of the desk or to fold their hands in their laps so that their attention is focused on you and what you have to say.

Guard Against Mix-Ups

An easy way to ensure that pieces do not get mixed up is to distribute manipulatives so that students seated next to each other have different colors. If one tangram piece should fall on the floor, it is easy to see whose it might be. If two students accidentally mix up their square tiles, different colors will allow them to easily sort them back into the original groups.

Institute a Class Clean-Up

Spend a few minutes at the end of the task having students help you put manipulatives back in proper order for the next use. Will you want to access them by color? In groups of 10? Have students count the pieces in the bags before zipping them shut. Ask them to restack connecting cubes into groups of 10 of a single color. Make counting and sorting manipulatives a natural part of the activity closure.

Organize It

Find a system to organize your classroom or school manipulatives so that they are readily available. Classroom teachers often store manipulatives in clear plastic bins or clear plastic bags so that the contents can be seen easily. Small pieces can be sorted and stored in tool or sewing boxes that have small compartments. Many schools store manipulatives in a central location and have sign-out systems to allow teachers to share them.

Sticky Notes

Following manipulative tasks, many teachers jot down observations and ideas regarding manipulative use to guide the next manipulative investigation. Placing reminder sticky notes in your plan book, teacher's manual, or on manipulative bags or containers will help you remember key management or activity ideas next time that manipulative is used.

Summary

Manipulatives are tools to help students visualize abstract concepts as well as tools to assist students in exploring math ideas or solving math problems. A variety of manipulatives, both store-bought and hand-made, are available for use within the classroom. Manipulatives motivate students, make math learning real and concrete, prompt discussions about math ideas, and allow teachers to see students at work doing mathematics.

Questions for Reflection

1. What is the role of the teacher before, during, and after a manipulative activity?
2. Which manipulatives can be used to demonstrate multiple concepts?
3. What types of management considerations are needed when using manipulatives?
4. How can manipulatives be stored and cataloged?
5. How can manipulatives be shared effectively within your school to allow for maximum use?

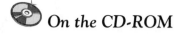 ## On the CD-ROM

Appendix B—Activities to Review Basic Math Facts and Computation Skills
Appendix C—Manipulative Templates

Suggested Resources

Bloomer, Anne, and Phyllis Carlson. 1992. *Activity Math: Using Manipulatives in the Classroom.* Lebanon, IN: Pearson Education.

Burns, Marilyn. 1992. *About Teaching Mathematics: A K–8 Resource, Second Edition.* Sausalito, CA: Math Solutions Publications.

Richardson, Kathy. 1999. *Developing Number Concepts: Planning Guide.* Lebanon, IN: Pearson Education.

Staff Development Training Videos

Burns, Marilyn. 2002. *Mathematics with Manipulatives.* Vernon Hills, IL: ETA/Cuisenaire.

Sources for Purchasing Classroom Manipulatives

ETA/Cuisenaire Company—
www.etacuisenaire.com
Lakeshore Learning Materials—
www.lakeshorelearning.com
Learning Resources—
www.learningresources.com

CHAPTER FOUR

Using Children's Literature to Teach Mathematics in Context

A significant factor in the development of students' understanding of mathematics is their recognition of when and how math is used in the world around them. Learning to apply skills and recognizing the meaningfulness of learning math skills are critical for generating motivation and enhancing students' conceptual understanding. Children's literature provides a context for learning math skills and offers engaging examples of their application.

Why Incorporate Children's Literature into Math Lessons?

Children love to read and hear stories! Regardless of grade level, students become engaged by stories and are magically transported to interesting settings, meet exciting characters, become entangled in fascinating problems, and work to figure out creative solutions. Stories allow students to follow a situation and reflect on ways that they might have handled that situation differently. Students gain insights through the exploits of characters within the story, as they applaud their wise actions or laugh at their mistakes. Stories engage children, and while they are engaged, students are open to learning.

Children's books show mathematics in action and allow students to experience math in real ways. Through listening to and reading stories in which mathematics' skills are presented, students see math being used to solve everyday problems. As students read about characters faced with problems that can be solved with math knowledge, they begin to see the usefulness of the skills they are learning. Books connect math to the real world.

The use of literature is valued as an effective technique for involving students as problem solvers, and provides a source for the development of classroom problems (Van de Walle 2004, Whitin and Whitin 2000). The story context engages students in problem-solving tasks in which they must reason and apply a variety of math skills. Once students are exposed to a math skill through a given scenario, it is easy for teachers to develop additional problems using the familiar characters and setting of the story.

Incorporating literature into the math classroom also provides students with practice in key communication skills (e.g., reading, talking, listening, writing). While some students struggle in their ability to communicate about abstract ideas in mathematics, the use of a story scenario often supports them in explaining their thinking and communicating their understanding. After listening to, reading, or discussing stories, students are able to respond verbally or in writing through answers to questions, reflections about their learning, and/or the development of related stories.

Students are intrinsically motivated by exploring math through stories (Griffiths and Clyne 1991), and studies have shown that the use of math-related children's literature has a positive effect on student dispositions toward math, as well as student math achievement (Hong 1996, Jennings et al. 1992).

Which Students Benefit from the Use of Math-Related Literature?

Bringing literature into the math classroom is beneficial at all grade levels. While we traditionally think of reading stories to young students, we recognize that all ages enjoy hearing stories. In *Sir Cumference and the First Round Table* by Cindy Neuschwander, the author uses humor and twists on mathematical terminology to challenge students' thinking; intermediate students will see the humor embedded in the story. In addition, their knowledge of math concepts helps them interpret story events. This picture book offers challenging ideas and intermediate-level humor.

In some cases, the same piece of literature can be used effectively for a variety of grade levels. At the primary level, *A Remainder of One* by Elinor J. Pinczes provides an example of a math concept (division with remainders) that students have not yet studied. At this level, students enjoy the story of poor soldier Joe, a bug who wants to march in a parade but must step aside each time the parade lines are uneven. Students' experiences with the story

help them develop some early knowledge about the concept of remainders (see Figure 4.1). In later grades, students benefit from the story as they struggle to understand the concept of division with remainders and need a context for the skill, and still older students enjoy the book as a review of the acquired concept or skill.

Various pieces of literature on the same topic can provide content information at a variety of levels to meet the needs of diverse students within the classroom. In class libraries, teachers can display books about geometry to meet the needs of students who are identifying shapes, those who are comparing characteristics of shapes, and others who are exploring more sophisticated geo-

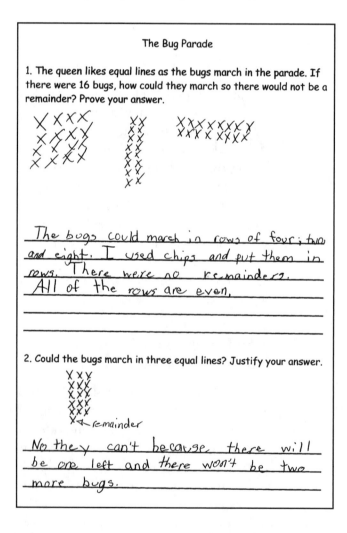

FIGURE 4.1 This third grader is able to understand and illustrate the concept of division with remainders after being introduced to the concept through a piece of literature.

metric concepts. Several carefully selected pieces of literature can provide choice at classroom centers (see Appendix K) and allow students to select a book that matches their skill level, reading level, or area of interest while all selections address a similar math topic.

How Can Teachers Select Appropriate Children's Literature for Math Lessons?

Using literature in the math classroom is more than just reading a story to students. It is about using that story to introduce, strengthen, or review a math idea. Selecting just the right book to achieve your goals is critical to the success of integrating literature into mathematics. Teachers have many choices as they look for books to meet the needs of their students and to mesh with their teaching objectives.

The selection of just the right piece of literature for a given lesson is an important instructional decision. When selecting a reading to use for a specific math lesson, consider the following questions.

- *Is the book or article of an appropriate reading/listening level for students?*— Select a book that is appropriate for the method in which you are sharing it with the class. If students will be doing the reading, be sure its reading level is appropriate. If you will be reading to the class, be sure that pictures are large enough to be seen and that students will understand the vocabulary and story events.

- *Does the math fit with the lesson?*—The mathematics represented in the story should blend with your objective for the lesson. A story about telling time to the half hour will not be the best choice for a lesson about elapsed time. Students need to be able to make sense of the math in the story in relation to the lesson. For a list of children's literature organized by math topic, see Appendix D.

- *Is the story engaging?*—Will the book engage and interest students? It should capture your students' interest enough to encourage them to think.

- *Do you enjoy the book?*—Selecting books you enjoy will allow you to pass that excitement on to students. If you like to read the book, your students will surely enjoy hearing it.

How Can Teachers Blend Literature into Math Lessons?

There are many options for when and how to incorporate math-related literature into classroom lessons. Teachers may choose to read aloud to students, have students read along with their own copy of books, or ask students to independently read the story. Books related to a math theme may be a part of a classroom library or a math center at which students independently read the story and engage in follow-up activities to review or extend their math skills. Students can individually explore books related to a math theme and complete projects related to that book. If teachers have multiple copies of a book, students as young as second grade can engage in a book study, discussing the math concepts appearing within the story and sharing their analysis of and reflections about the story. Math literature can also be a vehicle to review previously taught skills and concepts.

Books are a wonderful way to begin a lesson and to engage students in the topic or concept. The sharing of literature near the end of the lesson provides closure as students summarize their learning and discuss their understandings. Wherever you decide to place literature within your lesson, it should provide opportunities for discussion, exploration, and inquiry about mathematics. Discussing story events, writing about mathematical connections, and illustrating story concepts help students express their understanding. Manipulative activities in which students reenact or build on story events can also help strengthen their understanding of concepts.

The integration of mathematics and language arts objectives has gained popularity with teachers as they strive to demonstrate connections between various academic subjects. Selecting books that have a math focus, and also provide possibilities for the exploration of reading and language arts objectives, allows for a thematic, integrated instructional block. Students can explore a math concept with manipulatives, diagram the events of the story, and/or compare or contrast two characters. Objectives in math, language arts, and reading are merged as students explore the story. With proper planning, teachers can address objectives in both math and language arts, providing a natural flow to their lessons.

Students love to reread familiar stories. After sharing a book as a full-class read-aloud, consider placing it in the classroom library so that students can select it for independent reading (see Figure 4.2). Students often gravitate toward familiar stories or familiar characters. Once they have read Amy Axelrod's *Pigs Will Be Pigs*, they may become excited about exploring the other adventures of the pig family in her related titles. Recognizing familiar books or familiar characters is a great way to motivate students to continue reading on their own.

FIGURE 4.2   **This primary student enjoys rereading a math story that was shared with the class.**

What Is an Effective Framework for Planning Literature-Related Lessons?

Literature can be a fun and motivating way to begin or end a class session with the goal being a quick discussion or review of a math idea, or literature can be a part of a more complete lesson plan. If literature is to be a critical component to a more-developed lesson, the following before/during/after framework is a helpful way to organize the lesson (see this chapter's Classroom Ideas).

- Before-reading activities are done with students prior to the actual reading of a story. Such activities assess and activate prior knowledge, develop vocabulary or background information, and set a purpose for the reading.

- During-reading activities support students as they read or hear a story. Such activities encourage students to predict and to think through the events and support their comprehension of the story. During-reading activities are generally teacher prompts or questions to guide or stimulate student thinking as the story unfolds.

- After-reading activities reinforce and extend learning. Such activities provide students with opportunities to retell the story, to identify the math within the story, to discuss the story events, and to write about their understandings. After-reading activities use the context of the story to further develop mathematical ideas.

CLASSROOM IDEAS
Quick and Easy Literature Activities

As you plan for the use of math literature with students, consider a before-reading, during-reading, and after-reading lesson format. The following before, during, and after ideas will help you make the most of using literature in your math classroom.

Before Reading
Before-reading activities help to prepare students for the reading of the story and maximize their learning by focusing them on key ideas.

- *Set a context for the story*—Discuss the setting or ask a focusing question to get students thinking about a situation or event. A picture walk through the story—showing illustrations to get students thinking about and predicting story events—will help students focus on ideas that might help them understand the story better.

- *Highlight important vocabulary*—Consider which words within the story may be new to students. Introduce words that will impact students' understanding of the story.

- *Access or activate prior knowledge*—Ask questions to determine students' prior knowledge about the setting, scenario, or the math concept. Activate past knowledge with questions that remind students of previous skills or understandings.

- *Develop background knowledge*—Briefly share ideas or prompt discussions to develop knowledge that will help students better understand the math in the story.

- *Set a purpose for reading the story*—Prior to reading *The Doorbell Rang* by Pat Hutchins, you might say, "Today we are going to read a story about sharing. Let's see if everyone is happy about the way the cookies are shared." Before reading *Pigs Will Be Pigs* by Amy Axelrod, you might say, "Let's read to find out how the family raised enough money to eat at their favorite restaurant." Verbalizing a purpose for reading or listening to the story will help focus your students' attention on key story ideas.

During Reading
During-reading activities help keep students focused on the story and push them to process ideas and predict outcomes. On a first reading, limit questions and comments to those that will help students enjoy and process the story better. Too many questions may disturb the flow of the story and hinder students' understanding of the story as a whole. Remember that students enjoy hearing familiar stories, so rereading books will allow you to reexamine a story and ask further probing questions.

- *Ask students to predict events*—Before turning a page, ask for predictions about what characters might do or which math results might occur.

- *Ask focusing or probing questions to promote understanding*—Ask questions to get students to think about what they are hearing: "Should Anna have done that?" "How many candles do you think there will be?" "What will John need to know?"

After Reading
After-reading activities help students process ideas and explore math concepts. The following are some ways to help students further develop the concepts presented in stories.

CLASSROOM IDEAS (continued)
Quick and Easy Literature Activities

- *Identify the math*—Ask students to work with a partner to identify the math within the story. Have them share examples to support their ideas. In *Rooster's Off to See the World* by Eric Carle, they added animals as the rooster went on his journey, but then subtracted animals as each group decided to return home. As the children make chicken pens in *Chickens on the Move*, they need to understand both measurement and addition while exploring the concept of perimeter. You might ask students to put themselves in the position of a character in the story: "What math did that character need to know? Why?"

- *Act out the story using manipulatives*—Invite students to reenact a story's events with manipulatives. For *Grandfather Tang's Story* by Ann Tompert, students can use their own tangrams to create the changing shapes of the fox fairies throughout the story. For *Monster Math* by Grace Maccarone, students can use manipulatives to show the subtraction of the monsters one by one. For *Alexander Who Used to Be Rich Last Sunday* by Judith Viorst, students can use bags of money and subtract (remove) the correct amounts as Alexander spends or loses his money.

- *Pose comprehension questions*—Discuss a story's events or a character's actions following the reading of it. What was the problem? How was it solved? How did math help solve it? Focus on open-ended questions to guide students' inquiry into the story. Ask *why*, *how*, or *what if*. Discussions might be whole-class or teacher-directed, or they might be held in circles in which students talk about their predictions, pose questions, or retell the story to peers.

- *Continue the investigation*—Using a story's theme, present students with an investigation to further explore it. In *Two Ways to Count to Ten* retold by Ruby Dee, readers hear about the clever way the antelope counts to 10 (counting by 2s). Ask students to determine all of the possible ways to count to 20 or 40. In *A Cloak for the Dreamer* by Aileen Friedman, the tailor's third son finds that circles are not a good shape for creating a cloak because they cannot be sewn together so that there are no holes between them. Ask students to explore other shapes to determine which might be good shapes for creating a cloak with no holes (see Figure 4.3). *How Much Is a Million?* by David M. Schwartz is filled with problems about large numbers as Marvelosissimo the Mathematical Magician tells, among other things, how long

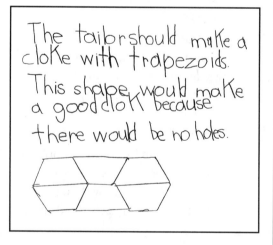

FIGURE 4.3   This second-grade student shares his ideas about a shape that would make a good cloak after hearing a related story.

CLASSROOM IDEAS (continued)
Quick and Easy Literature Activities

it would take to count from one to one million. Ask students how they might figure out the height of 100 math books stacked on top of each other. Have them explain their plan for solving the problem.

■ *Explore similar experiences*—Ask students to work in groups to think about times when they may have had similar experiences. Have they been late for activities like Max in *It's About Time, Max!* by Kitty Richards? Have they measured items with a tape measure like Carrie in *Carrie Measures Up* by Linda Williams Aber? Discuss the similarities between students' experiences and the experiences of the characters in stories.

■ *Create math problems*—Use the story context to come up with problems, or ask students to create problems about the story (see Figure 4.4). In *Counting on Frank* by Rod Clement, the boy knocks peas off his plate. If the boy accidentally knocks 15 peas off his plate each night, how many peas would he knock off in one week? In *Amanda Bean's Amazing Dream* by Cindy Neuschwander, 7 grandmas were knitting sweaters. If each grandma knitted 7 sweaters and each sweater had 5 buttons, how many buttons were there? In *Pigs Will Be Pigs* by Amy Axelrod, the Pig family found money to use for dinner at their favorite restaurant. If you found $12.00, use the menu in the Axelrod book to decide what you would order at the restaurant? Then, use math data to prove that you will have enough money. Problems, such as the one in Figure 4.4, might be used for class warm-ups or students might try to stump partners with their problems.

■ *Write a similar story*—Ask students to write a story of their own with a similar style or theme. If they are reading a counting book with a special theme, such as *Feast for 10!* by Cathryn Falwell, ask students to create a counting book with a different theme. If they are reading a story with a chance and probability theme, such as in *Bad Luck Brad* by Gail Herman, ask students to write a story about someone who has a chance of winning a prize. If they are reading a story in which characters organize data to solve a problem, such as in *The Best Vacation Ever* by Stuart J. Murphy, ask students to write a story about a family who charts a different type of decision. The shared story becomes a model for students as they create similar stories.

Our Lemondade Stand

You are having a lemonade stand to make money for a class field trip to a pizza restaurant. For the stand, you will need:

■ 4 lbs. of lemons
■ 3 lbs. of sugar
■ 2 lbs. of ice
■ 100 cups

The cost of these items is:

■ Lemons - $1.00 lb.
■ Sugar - $1.50 lb.
■ Ice - $0.25 lb.
■ Cups - $2.25 for 100

1. What were your expenses? How much did they cost?
2. If you sold 100 cups of lemonade for 25 cents each, how much profit did you make?

FIGURE 4.4   This sixth grader created a math problem about expenses and profit after reading a story that developed those concepts.

Summary

A critical component for developing students' understanding of mathematics is their recognition of when and how math is used. Children's literature provides students with examples; the use of a story context supports problem-solving instruction and helps develop students' reasoning and communication skills. Students can explore math concepts within a story's context through a variety of before-reading, during-reading, and after-reading activities. The sharing of math-related children's literature provides motivation, encourages engagement, and adds meaningfulness to math lessons.

Questions for Reflection

1. How can introducing and exploring mathematics concepts through children's literature foster a deeper understanding of the concepts?
2. In what ways does the use of children's literature provide a context for problem-solving activities? Share some examples.
3. How can the use of children's literature support the needs of students of varying abilities within the same classroom?
4. Can the objectives of mathematics and language arts be met within a single lesson? What are the implications for lesson planning?

On the CD-ROM

Appendix D—Children's Literature Related to Math Concepts
Appendix K—Math Centers

Suggested Resources

Braddon, Kathryn L., Nancy J. Hall, and Dale Taylor. 1993. *Math Through Children's Literature*. Englewood, CO: Teacher Ideas Press.

Bresser, Rusty. 1995. *Math and Literature, Grades 4–6*. Sausalito, CA: Math Solutions Publications.

Burns, Marilyn. 1992. *Math and Literature (K–3) Book One*. Sausalito, CA: Math Solutions Publications.

Griffiths, Rachel, and Margaret Clyne. 1991. *Books You Can Count On*. Portsmouth, NH: Heinemann.

Thiessen, Diane. 2004. *Exploring Mathematics Through Literature*. Reston, VA: National Council of Teachers of Mathematics.

Welchman-Tischler, Rosamond. 1992. *How to Use Children's Literature to Teach Mathematics*. Reston, VA: National Council of Teachers of Mathematics.

Whitin, David, and Sandra Wilde. 1992. *Read Any Good Math Lately? Children's Books for Mathematical Learning, K–6*. Portsmouth, NH: Heinemann.

CHAPTER FIVE

Guiding Understanding Through Teacher Talk

This chapter explores the power of a teacher's words—"teacher talk"—in guiding students to a deeper understanding of mathematics. Teacher talk might consist of questions, information, insights, and examples through which he or she informs, models, and demonstrates concepts and ideas. Teacher talk might take the form of carefully crafted questions that guide whole-class discussions, group work, or individual learning. Teacher talk might include providing directions for class activities or comments to guide and monitor students' attitudes and behaviors.

Traditionally, mathematics teachers shared information through a lecture-style approach to instruction and then asked questions of students to get answers—the right answers. Today, teacher talk looks very different in many math classrooms across the country. By modeling our own thinking, facilitating whole-class and small-group discussions, and posing carefully selected questions to guide and assess the development of ideas, we are using our words to facilitate understanding rather than simply to articulate content.

Why Ask Questions in the Math Classroom?

Teacher questioning behaviors are very much related to increases in student achievement (Collins and Mangieri 1992, Gall 1984, Redfield and Rosseau 1981). Although teachers tend to ask recall questions more frequently than they ask higher-order questions, research shows that the higher-order questions (e.g., those that ask students to apply, analyze, and reason) produce more learning than questions that focus simply on recall of information (Marzano, Pickering, and Pollock 2001). Questions that go beyond factual recall and require them to think more thoroughly about a topic arouse students' curiosity and spark their thinking and reasoning skills. Leinwand (2000) contends that the best way to implement a thinking curriculum, to focus students on alternate approaches, and to create a language-rich classroom is by regularly asking "Why?" or "How do you know?" or "Can you explain what you did and why you did it?"

Routinely reflecting on their learning assists students in acquiring new knowledge (Fennema and Romberg 1999). Conceptual understanding is developmental; we build on knowledge by linking new concepts to existing knowledge. A key purpose of questioning is to help students connect what they are learning to what they already know. Asking questions (e.g., "What does this remind you of?" "When have we done this before?" "What do we know about . . .?") helps guide students as they link what they know to what they are learning.

Being able to articulate ideas is an indicator of understanding (Fennema and Romberg 1999, Corwin 1996). Students must recognize and understand essential ideas so that they can communicate about their knowledge. Posing questions to explore in whole-class or small-group settings provides students with experience in contemplating and articulating ideas. Questions can help bring struggling students to an understanding of a concept or can push an advanced student to delve more fully into a concept. Students may initially struggle to articulate their thoughts, but articulation improves as they sort out ideas and fine-tune their communication skills.

Which Questions Support the Development of Mathematical Thinking?

When teaching for understanding in math, questions become a key to guiding the development of that understanding. Questions that ask for literal knowledge are used frequently; however, questions that probe for more than a literal understanding have tremendous value as both an instructional tool and an assessment technique. The answer to "How many sides does a square have?" provides us with a different level of assessment than does the answer to "How are squares and rectangles alike? How are they different?"; the latter one pushes students to think and communicate at a higher level.

There are a variety of reasons to ask questions in the math classroom. Questioning is an instructional tool that can impact both process (how students learn) and content (what students learn). As a process tool, questions can

engage students in the activity ("When was the last time you . . . ?"), spark student-to-student discussions ("What do you think about what Dan said?"), and help to clarify processes ("Who can explain what your group needs to do?"). As a tool to develop content understanding, questions can challenge students' thinking ("But what if . . . ?") and help students make connections ("What does this remind you of?"). Questions can guide the development of ideas ("So what might that tell you about . . . ?") and probe for reasoning, predictions, and problem solving ("Why do you believe . . . ?"). Recognizing why you are asking questions will help you choose the right questions to ask. The questioning categories in Figure 5.1 can be used to facilitate the generation of a variety of thought-provoking questions.

Teachers can pose questions to the whole class to assist students in focusing on a topic prior to a lesson, to help students process information during a lesson, or to assist them in summarizing learning at the end of a lesson. Teacher questioning can support group activities as teachers provide specific questions to guide each group's work and to push group members to an increased understanding of the task or problem. Questioning also can support individual students as teachers kneel next to them to ask questions to gauge their understanding, redirect their efforts, or revise their thinking.

Some questioning is designed to lead students to insights. Rather than telling a primary student that her pattern is inaccurate, the teacher might ask a series of questions, such as the following, to lead the student to correct her own work.

"What is the pattern?"
"What part repeats?"
"Show me the part that repeats."
"So what would come next?"

A fifth-grade student was asked to find the sum of .5 and .7 and found the answer to be .12. The teacher chose to use questions to probe the student's thinking.

Questions can ask students to . . .

Clarify Ideas and Procedures

Can you restate that in your own words?

Are you saying . . . ?

Can someone tell me what you will be doing in your groups?

Who can describe the procedures for working at the math center?

Compare and/or Contrast Ideas or Concepts

How is _____ like _____? How is it different?

What are the similarities between _____ and _____?

What are the differences between _____ and _____?

Connect Ideas to Other Ideas

What does this remind you of?

When have we seen something like this before?

What are some real-world examples of _____ ?

How could you use this math idea in your life?

How is this related to what we did last week?

Explain a Process

How did you solve that problem?

What steps did you use to _____?

Justify a Solution or Process

Why is that the answer?

Why do you believe . . . ?

Why did you do it that way?

Which is better? Why?

Prove that your answer is correct.

Why is that an appropriate strategy to solve the problem?

Observe and Draw Conclusions

What observations did you make?

What did you notice about _____?

What conclusion can you draw?

Predict an Outcome

Estimate the answer. Explain your estimate.

About how many _____ will fit in _____?

What do you think the answer would be if _____ ?

Probe for Further Ideas

So, how could we build on that idea?

What is your plan for solving this problem?

Who can answer Brendan's question?

Reflect on Thinking (Metacognition)

How did you figure that out?

How did you get your answer?

Describe what you were thinking.

What was difficult about that concept?

Respond to Others' Ideas

Will Allison's plan work?

Do you agree with Jason?

State Information and/or Recall Ideas

What is a _____?

Tell me what _____ means.

What are the characteristics of _____?

Describe a _____.

Summarize Ideas

Can you summarize what we learned?

What are the key ideas?

FIGURE 5.1

TEACHER: "How much is .5? What would be another way to say that?"

KELLY: "It's like half."

TEACHER: "About how much is .7?"

KELLY: "More than half."

TEACHER: "About how much is .12?"

KELLY: "About 12 out of 100."

TEACHER: "Is that more or less than half?"

KELLY: "A lot less"

TEACHER: "Does that make sense?"

KELLY: "No—I mean, it should be more than half."

TEACHER: "What might make sense?"

KELLY: "More than one whole because they both are a half or more than a half."

Through a series of questions that guided her thinking, the teacher helped Kelly realize the unreasonableness of her first answer.

What Will Help Improve Questioning Techniques?

To make the most of questioning in the classroom, it is important to reflect on question selection, how to pose questions, which students to direct questions to, what behavior to display while waiting for student responses, and what comments to make in response to students' verbalizations. Reflecting on these issues allows us to pinpoint ways to improve the use of questioning with students.

Selecting thoughtful questions is the starting point. Avoid concentrating on questions that ask for literal understanding. Pose questions that may have more than one right answer and that require students to think and verbalize about that thinking. Ask the "how" and "why" questions and prompt students to elaborate in their responses. Whether right or wrong, ask students to explain and justify their ideas. Encourage student-to-student discussions by asking students to respond to each other's questions or to comment on each other's thoughts. Be sure questions are phrased clearly, because their clarity will significantly impact students' ability to respond appropriately.

Create an environment in which students are willing to take risks and to offer comments even if they are not sure of their correctness. Demonstrate to students the importance of listening to each other. Welcome debates. Celebrate surprises and discoveries. Model that even the teacher does not always have the answer and may need to observe, investigate, and amend his or her thinking to find the answer. Be willing to refrain from deeming answers right or wrong—so that students can ponder ideas and come back to them later with additional insight.

What Is the Role of Discussion in the Math Classroom?

Classroom discussions help students delve more fully into problems and allow them to share ideas and discover new ideas (Whitin and Whitin 2000). Students often use intuitive knowledge to solve problems before they are taught basic skills. Facilitating discussions about their actions and posing thoughtful questions often helps them realize what they've done. Sigmund Freud said "When inspiration does not come to me, I go halfway to meet it." Questioning is a key tool to help students meet inspiration because questions gently guide their insights and conclusions. Along with playing a key role in the recognition and development of strategies for solving problems, discussions are also important in helping students develop number sense, estimation strategies, and invented strategies for computations (Van de Walle 2004).

Whole-class and small-group discussions allow opportunities for students to hear others' thinking, express their own ideas, and combine what they know with what they hear to clarify and refine their thinking. "Through communication, ideas become objects of reflection, refinement, discussion, and amendment" (NCTM 2000, 60). The teacher, as the facilitator of discussions, works to pull ideas from students and poses questions to stimulate reflection, build connections, and encourage reasoning and conjecture.

Whole-class discussions provide students with the opportunity to defend their thinking. They also provide teachers with opportunities for summarization of ideas and are a natural lesson closure activity through prompts such as "What did you learn today?" Whole-class discussions allow students to debrief on strategies or solutions, a critical step in developing effective problem solvers. As students share strategies and solutions, teachers probe into the decisions they made as they worked through the problem, as well as the difficulties encountered during the problem-solving process. Through whole-class discussions, students learn what is acceptable in terms of justifications or explanations as the teacher probes for more details or missing steps. Primary students may need more support during discussions as they learn to see other points of view and fold others' ideas into their own understandings. Whole-class discussions encourage responses without penalty of being wrong and allow all students to share ideas. Insights are celebrated, and misunderstandings are considered a part of the process.

Facilitating whole-class discussions is a skill that takes some time to develop. Multiple students should be given an opportunity to respond, but discussions shouldn't drag on so that others lose interest. Keep the pace moving and keep students involved in the discussion. Questions and comments should provide transitions between students' comments and need to highlight key ideas everyone should hear. Having students' respond to each others' comments will help keep them focused on the topic, and opportunities to share with partners in the midst of whole-class discussions will keep everyone involved.

In small-group discussions, the teacher moves through the classroom to monitor and guide the student thinking in each group. During such work, the teacher may join a group to question ideas or to clarify information or perhaps redirect or challenge a small group. The teacher uses questioning techniques to check for understanding while rotating between groups. Often when circulating through the room during small-group discussions, teachers hear insights from one group that might benefit others or recognize that a few groups need to be redirected. Calling a class "time-out" allows teachers to pull everyone back together to discuss ideas, clarify procedures, and assist or extend learning. Asking questions during time-outs offers groups the opportunity to share their ideas with others in the room. After sharing some ideas, the teacher can then direct the class to get back to the small-group discussions.

What Is the Role of Modeling and Demonstrating in the Math Classroom?

Teacher modeling and demonstrating can be quite powerful instructional tools when implemented well; however, many teacher demonstrations fail to reach students in the way that was anticipated. Many of us probably remember teachers demonstrating the steps in a math process on a blackboard but were still unable to understand or remember those steps. We have learned that just telling students how to do a math process is not likely to yield the expected results for all students; just seeing what to do does not always result in being able to do it. Being a mathematician means being able to think through situations and to make sense of problems. Mathematicians recognize that getting stuck is a part of the math process, and that they need to build strategies for getting themselves "unstuck." What teachers are thinking is what they want to convey to students during demonstrations, not just what to do, but why to do it. Modeling and demonstrating, combined with think-aloud techniques and student questioning, are powerful tools that will meet the needs of most students.

The use of visuals during teacher demonstrations is essential. Mathematical ideas can be very abstract and many students need to see models to truly understand them. At times, we choose to give all students manipulatives to explore ideas in a concrete way. At other times, we may decide to model ideas through whole-class demonstrations so that students can see and hear the thinking as mathematical experiences are modeled. Visual demonstrations might be conducted with accompanying pictures, symbols, or numbers on a board or overhead projector. Teachers should verbalize as they record the diagrams or equations. The combination of visual and verbal cues helps all students make sense of ideas. Overhead versions are available for most types of manipulatives, from pattern blocks to geoboards to base-ten blocks to spinners or dice. Video visualizers allow students to see the teacher, or a student volunteer, manipulate concrete materials while math ideas are explained or explored. Many teachers create hand-made manipulatives to tape on boards or stick to magnetic boards (see Figure 5.2).

How Do Think-Aloud Techniques Enhance Modeling and Demonstrating?

A think-aloud is a technique in which teachers verbalize their thoughts and actions as they solve a math problem or explain a math con-

cept. Think-alouds are more than just verbalizing the steps to solve a problem; they include verbalizations of the thinking that otherwise would not be visible to the students. Teachers can verbalize reasoning ("I think I'll start with this number because. . . "), confusion ("That answer doesn't make sense!"), or insight ("Oh, now I see what is happening here!"). Think-alouds show students that all mathematicians get confused at times, but that effective ones find a plan for figuring out how to proceed with a problem. Think-alouds give teachers a vehicle for showing students how they plan for solving problems, react to setbacks during the problem-solving process, and monitor the reasonableness of their solutions.

Keene and Zimmermann (1997) identified strategies that can be effectively modeled through think-alouds, including predicting, clarifying, visualizing, using prior knowledge, building new connections, summarizing, and synthesizing. While their ideas are set in the context of reading instruction, the ideas are applicable to mathematics content. As the teacher shares comments, such as the following, students begin to see what is happening inside his head as he explores mathematics.

I'm guessing that . . .
I predict . . .
I wonder whether . . .
I am trying to figure out . . .
I need to know . . .
I visualized . . .
This reminds me of . . .
This is like when we . . .
So far, I know that . . .
This gives me an idea . . .
I tried this, but . . .
I had a hard time with this part . . .
This answer doesn't seem to make sense because . . .

Students can be prompted to model the teacher's think-aloud techniques as they work with partners, sharing what they've done and why they've done it as they work together to solve problems. Think-alouds make thinking visible and provide students with a model of

FIGURE 5.2   This teacher provides visuals as she explores a combination problem with her students.

the kinds of questions, concerns, and insights that occur to mathematicians as they explore ideas.

How Can Teachers Create an Environment to Promote Discourse?

To have fruitful discussions, it is important to create a climate that is safe and nonthreatening. The teacher should set the tone for respecting and welcoming all students' comments. While some students readily volunteer ideas, others may be reluctant to share their thoughts. Prior to asking students to share ideas with the entire class, partner sharing will stimulate ideas for students who struggle to express their thoughts. When teachers pose questions that can have multiple responses (e.g., "What things in our classroom are shaped like a rectangular prism?"), hesitant students or low achievers can be asked to respond first before the more obvious examples have been given. This will allow them to participate and begin to build their confidence.

Another factor in promoting discourse is the responses teachers give to students' remarks. Through responses to their comments, students can either shut down or reflect on their ideas and learn from them. It is important for all students to feel that their contributions to class discussions are valued. Teachers must model the ability to listen to ideas, to respect ideas, to reevaluate and modify ideas, and to initially accept errors in thinking. Students will learn to respect others' ideas if their ideas are respected.

Sometimes students' responses are wrong, off-topic, or confusing. It can be challenging to figure out positive ways to respond to their comments, ways that will encourage them to

continue contributing to the discussions. Consider using some of the following options.

Partially Correct or Emerging Answers
"You're almost there."
"That's part of it."

Putting an Answer on Hold
"We'll come back to that idea."
"Think about it and we'll come back to you."
"Can someone help . . ."

Probing Comments
"What else?"
"Tell us more."
"Why?"
"What do you mean by that?"
"Can you give me an example of what you mean?"

Plus, remember the power of nonverbal feedback. Your smiles, gestures, energy, and eye contact can convey warmth and acceptance, which will help students feel comfortable about sharing their thoughts.

While often a challenge, we need to listen and respond to students' ideas rather than wait for a preconceived answer. A student may have wonderful insights or a correct response even when the answer is not the one expected. In addition, listening to students' errors tells us a great deal about what they do and do not understand. Students need to feel free to take risks and share their ideas, even if they are not sure of their validity. In classrooms that promote discourse, teachers and students acknowledge wrong answers as part of the learning process, listen to each others' thinking, and celebrate insights and discoveries.

CLASSROOM IDEAS
Quick and Easy Questioning Activities

Slow It Down

Allow sufficient wait time (3–5 seconds) after asking questions. The quality of answers improves and the quantity of students who respond increases with proper wait time. Be willing to wait for students to formulate ideas and give them time to finish their thoughts before commenting.

Elicit Multiple Responses

When asking for a response from students, don't stop after just one response, even if the answer is correct. Ask several other students to share their answers. It will benefit students to hear explanations and justifications verbalized in a variety of ways. And, it will allow students to hear and test a variety of answers before they make up their minds which answer they believe to be correct.

Call on All Students Equitably

Create an environment where every student wants to be heard and every student gets the opportunity to be heard. Are you more likely to call on students seated in a certain part of the room? Do you have a tendency to call on students of a certain ability level, race, or gender? Try a technique for random name-calling (e.g., placing students' names on index cards and selecting a card at random).

Think-Pair-Share

Frank Lyman's Think-Pair-Share strategy is a simple technique that yields positive results (Kagan 1992). The technique has the combined benefits of wait time and partner- and whole-group sharing. The teacher poses a question and students are asked to *think* about their response; this is a silent time when all hands are down. Next, students are asked to *pair* with a partner and discuss the response, then they are asked to *share* their responses in a whole-class discussion. Lyman's strategy allows all students to be involved in the activity rather than just the one or two quick-responding students who might be called on in traditional question-and-answer sessions. It also provides everyone with the opportunity to hear others' thinking and to develop responses, even if they did not have a quick answer after the teacher posed the question. This technique encourages all students to participate in thinking and talking about math and allows reluctant students to refine ideas in a less-threatening partner setting to gain the confidence to voice them to the entire class (see Figure 5.3). Think-Pair-Share prompts include the following.

- How will you solve this problem? Or, how did you solve this problem?
- What are odd numbers? What are even numbers?
- Why is estimation important?
- Why is mental math important? When have you done mental math?

FIGURE 5.3 Working with partners prompts students to verbalize their ideas and allows them to hear others' ideas.

CLASSROOM IDEAS (*continued*)
Quick and Easy Questioning Activities

▌ When might you need to understand how to divide?

▌ Name some items that show symmetry.

A Think-Pair-Square variation has students sharing in groups of four after they have paired with their partners (Kagan 1992).

Show It

Use manipulatives during demonstrations to provide a visual as you explain ideas (for templates, see Appendix C). There are a wide variety of transparent manipulatives that are perfect for demonstrations on an overhead projector. Having them organized and close to the projector so that they are available for spontaneous demonstrations is important. Try using a sewing box, a fishing tackle box, a tool kit, or a desk organizer to store overhead manipulatives; that way each type of manipulative (or color or size) can be stored in separate sections for easy access.

Student-Generated Questions

Encourage students to construct questions of their own about math topics. Talk about types of questions and challenge students to design their own. When asking questions in class, you might occasionally follow the question with "Why did I ask that question?" As students respond—"Because you wanted to know if I knew the steps to doing ___" or

"Because you wanted to know if I knew what that word meant" or "Because you wanted to know if I could come up with data to back up my answer"—they are becoming more cognizant of why questions are being asked. Helping students identify the purpose of questions will support them as they design their own questions. Primary students might work as a class to come up with math questions about a story they have read together. Intermediate students might be asked to work with a partner to design questions to review a unit of study.

Interviews

Teachers frequently conduct individual writing or reading conferences; how about individual math conferences? While the class is working on an assigned task, teachers have opportunities to conduct brief student interviews. The interview might last for just a couple minutes, but it allows the teacher to ask questions to hear an individual student's thinking. A teacher might choose to interview just a few students who appear to be struggling with a skill to be better able to assess their level of understanding, or he or she might decide to rotate through the classroom over a period of days to interview a larger number of students. Interviews are an invaluable assessment tool.

Summary

Teacher talk is the underpinning of solid instruction. A teacher's words guide the sharing of thoughts and information during modeling and demonstrations, facilitate the give-and-take of ideas during whole-class discussions, guide the collaboration of students during group activities, prompt struggling individuals, and challenge advanced learners. Communication about ideas is what moves mathematics from a focus on isolated skills to a focus on understanding. Discussions about problems and procedures elevate the level of students' thinking from rote to conceptual.

On the CD-ROM

Appendix C—Manipulative Templates

Suggested Resources

Chapin, Suzanne H., Catherine O'Connor, and Nancy Canavan Anderson. 2003. *Classroom Discussions: Using Math Talk to Help Students Learn.* Sausalito, CA: Math Solutions Publications.

Corwin, Rebecca B. 1996. *Talking Mathematics— Supporting Children's Voices.* Portsmouth, NH: Heinemann.

Griffiths, Rachel, and Margaret Clyne. 1994. *Language in the Mathematics Classroom.* Portsmouth, NH: Heinemann.

Sullivan, Peter, and Pat Lilburn. 2002. *Good Questions for Math Teaching: Why Ask Them and What to Ask, Grades K–6.* Sausalito, CA: Math Solutions Publications.

Questions for Reflection

1. What types of questions should you ask in math class? (Record yourself during a class period and transcribe the questions you ask.)
2. How many responses do you allow? Do you encourage students to respond to each other?
3. What is your comfort level when students are unable to answer the questions you pose? What do you do next?
4. What is the value of whole-class discussions? Small-group discussions?
5. How do demonstrations and think-alouds support the development of math understanding?
6. In what ways can you encourage all students to share their ideas?

CHAPTER SIX

Developing the Language of Math

Language plays a key role in a classroom focused on mathematical understanding. Students' ability to understand the language of mathematics impacts their knowledge about its concepts, as well as their ability to express ideas about content. This chapter explores the role of vocabulary in helping students understand math content and communicate their mathematical ideas.

Why Focus on Math Vocabulary?

Understanding the meaning of words within a content area is a critical component of learning that content because it is through language that meaning is conveyed (Moore et al. 1994). Specialized math vocabulary, including symbols and abbreviations, is not a part of students' everyday experiences and must be developed within the classroom so that students can understand and use the appropriate words and symbols as they process the information and communicate about the various math concepts (Griffiths and Clyne 1994). The amount of vocabulary related to math is staggering (see Appendix E). With so many new words, often with multiple meanings, emphasizing the development of students' vocabulary becomes a critical component of the elementary math program.

Research studies (Marzano, Pickering, and Pollock 2001) indicate the benefits of vocab-

ulary instruction, including its positive impact on the comprehension of new content. Introduction to and practice with new math words allows students to become familiar with them, process their meanings, and use words appropriately as they communicate about mathematics. Because students often struggle to find just the right word to express their mathematical thinking, a better math vocabulary can enhance their ability to accurately pinpoint and convey meaning.

Why Is Learning Math Vocabulary a Challenge for Students?

When students enter school, they experience a new language as they begin to learn mathematics; new words are introduced as each new concept is explored. Many new words! Some are familiar words that now have new meanings related to mathematics. Primary students hear the words *feet* or *yard* and intermediate students hear the words *mean* or *volume* as we talk about math concepts. Knowing the common meanings does not help students understand the new way in which these words are being used in mathematics. Attention to the math meanings of words clarifies students' confusions and leads to their greater ability to understand the language of math.

Along with familiar words with new meanings, there are words that are unique to the study of mathematics. Students rarely hear the words *symmetry,* *exponent,* or *decimal* at home; these generally are words heard just in the math classroom. Students' only exposure to such words may be during the short time they spend in math class.

With each new concept come many more math words. The understanding of these words, and students' later ability to use them as they explain and describe their mathematical thinking, becomes a critical foundation for students' conceptual development. As with any new language, students need opportunities to hear and speak it to make the words their own; students need to be actively involved in speaking and writing this new language to internalize the words so that they can use them.

How Can Students' Math Vocabulary Be Expanded?

Vocabulary is developed when students are introduced to new words and given opportunities to use those words. When copying a definition from a dictionary or glossary, I often had as much trouble understanding the definition as the word itself. This activity does not help students learn new words because definitions get copied without even thinking about meanings. Teachers' regular use of specific math vocabulary during discussions and demonstrations helps improve students' knowledge in a natural way. Classroom discussions that are interactive—requiring students to both talk and listen—help them develop vocabulary in a meaningful way. However, teachers must also provide specific opportunities for students to explore the multitude of new words and terms presented with each new math domain. In their review of research on vocabulary development, Marzano, Pickering, and Pollock (2001) suggest that vocabulary instruction should include repeated exposure to words, instruction in new words, visual images to enhance retention of words, and a focus on those words that are critical to content.

For students to learn to speak the language of math, teacher planning should include attention to language objectives as well as content objectives. Teachers who make note of new words that are being introduced and plan activities to explore the meanings of those words ensure that students will build a foundation for both communication and conceptual understanding. Regardless of grade level, vocabulary activities enhance the development of math concepts and can be easily integrated into mathematics lessons.

Providing frequent opportunities for students to talk together is important for enhancing their vocabularies. Frequent cooperative learning activities provide students with the opportunity to hear others' ideas, as well as the words they choose to express those ideas. Activities can be simple (e.g., "Turn to your partner and discuss whether this shape has a line of symmetry." "Describe this geometric shape to your partner using math vocabulary."). Teachers who rotate through the classroom during group work have a great opportunity to stimulate vocabulary development. While monitoring activities, teachers can listen for interesting vocabulary to share with the entire group (e.g., "In this group I heard someone say . . ." "Group 2 had an interesting way to describe . . .").

Introducing new vocabulary can be as simple as displaying new words on the board or an overhead, then engaging students in discussions in which the word is used in context. Lists of words related to specific math concepts can be generated. Word walls or vocabulary logs are techniques for students to see and record new words. Math games that require an understanding of math vocabulary provide ongoing opportunities to enhance students' use of math words (see Appendix B). Activities can be quick and easy for the teacher and still provide enriching opportunities for students to "talk math." Just spending a few minutes with word work at the start or end of a class period will greatly benefit students, and activities are easily integrated into the math topic being studied.

Developing vocabulary in context is critical (NCTM 2000). When exploring probability, for example, you might ask students to work in groups to create a web of probability words. When focusing on measurement, you might ask students to write measurement riddles to strengthen both concepts and vocabulary. When exploring fractions, students might be asked to sort and categorize a group of fraction words. As students explore mathematics, it is important to provide opportunities for them to learn and to use the language as they communicate about their mathematical thinking.

Many teachers have found vocabulary logs to be a valuable tool for students to record the words they are learning; words can be organized alphabetically or by math topic. As students learn new words, they are discussed in class, then students are asked to record the words and their meanings in a log (see Figure 6.1). Students reword glossary definitions so that they are understandable to them and may add a diagram or example that helps them remember a word's meaning. Vocabulary logs are meant to be used as a reference to assist students in correctly choosing and using math vocabulary during writing tasks. (For ideas about math writing, see Appendix H.)

Attention to the connection between reading and writing will help students discover tools to find the meaning of words they do not understand. As students read the math text, assisting them with the use of context clues to determine meanings, or helping them use the glossary, word boxes, diagrams, and other conventions of expository text, will facilitate expanded vocabularies. Particularly for upper-elementary students, an understanding of expository text features (e.g., glossary, index, headings, diagrams) will help them not only in their understanding of math words but also will serve as a model of how to effectively express mathematical ideas.

What Is the Role of Word Walls in Mathematics?

Word walls are displays of math vocabulary words that are built or constructed collaboratively with students (see Figure 6.2). These displays of key words are posted in an organized way on a classroom wall or bulletin board. In mathematics, word walls can be used at all grade levels to provide opportunities for students to see and use key words and to foster their ability to read and write about mathematical ideas. They provide reference support and independence during their writing about math and allow students to develop

FIGURE 6.1 This intermediate student expresses his understanding of parallel and intersecting lines using his own words, examples, and pictures.

FIGURE 6.2 Word walls are instructional tools. This student has found a word based on a clue given by the teacher.

an extensive vocabulary that provides the foundation for mathematical communication. Word walls are instructional tools, not classroom decorations, that allow students to visualize words, see connections between words, and explore word meanings. Students interact with words on the wall as they learn them.

How Should Word Walls Be Developed?

Locating just the right place for a word wall is important. The location should allow the words to be easily seen by students as they engage in writing tasks. Words should be written in bold letters and be large enough for students to see from their seats.

Words should be introduced gradually and walls built with students' help. To build a "wall," a teacher might write the new word on chart paper, sentence strip, or paper "brick." The word can be used in a sentence, students can be asked to brainstorm its meaning or to provide an example to show their understanding of the word. Older students might be asked how they figured out the meaning and challenged to explain the strategy that helped them "decode" the word. As each word is introduced, the teacher and students discuss it as it relates to other known math words or concepts, then the teacher places the word in an appropriate place on the wall.

Primary-grade classrooms often have one large word wall, which is organized alphabetically with words from all content areas; however, a separate math word wall will work for all grade levels. Word walls can be based on a unit or concept in math (e.g., addition, geometry, measurement) and also may include math symbols. Providing picture support is helpful for many words. A picture of a *pentagon*, a *right angle*, or *parallel lines* placed next to the words will help students remember and retain meanings. If there is not enough wall space, word walls can be created on cabinets, rolling carts, cardboard trifolds, or white boards. If there are too many words to keep them posted throughout the year, teachers can have students record each new word and meaning in their math vocabulary logs for reference.

How Can Teachers Use Word Walls as Instructional Tools?

Providing frequent opportunities for students to refer to and interact with words on the word wall will ensure that they see the wall as a resource for writing and talking about math ideas. Teachers might ask students to draw pictures to show their understanding of the words on the wall or to create riddles for some of them. Teachers might say a sentence but omit a math term and ask students to try to guess which word is missing. The teacher might mention a topic to the class (e.g., multiplication) and ask students to find all of the words on the wall that connect to it. Even when teachers have just brief periods of time (e.g., a few quick minutes before students need to line up for lunch), it is possible to turn the word wall into an instructional activity. Teachers might give a clue, then ask students to find the word to go with the clue (e.g., "I am thinking of the word that means a shape with three sides and three corners."). Providing various opportunities to interact with the words on the wall will help students become familiar with and develop a greater understanding of them.

CLASSROOM IDEAS
Quick and Easy Vocabulary Activities

Word Webs

In this easy-to-implement activity, students work in pairs or groups to brainstorm and record words related to a math term (see Figures 6.3 and 6.4). If the key word is *measurement*, primary students might add *feet*, *yards*, *miles*, *pounds*, *ruler*, *yardstick*, *scale*, and/or *measuring cup*. Older students might add *volume*, *capacity*, *linear*, *thermometer*, *trundle wheel*, and/or *pedometer*. After allowing students several minutes to work with a partner or team, the teacher might compile a class word web on an overhead, board, or chart paper. This is a valuable way to check prior knowledge before beginning a unit or to summarize words learned at the end of a unit.

The class web may be posted throughout a unit so that the class can add new words as they learn them.

Sort and Label

Students are provided with a list of words from a math unit. They are then asked to work with a partner or group to sort the words into categories and decide on a title or label, which should tell how the items are alike or related, for each group. Students are then asked to share and justify their groupings. (*Note:* There is no "correct" way to group the words. Groupings should make sense for the words given. If students are unable to find a group for a word, they can

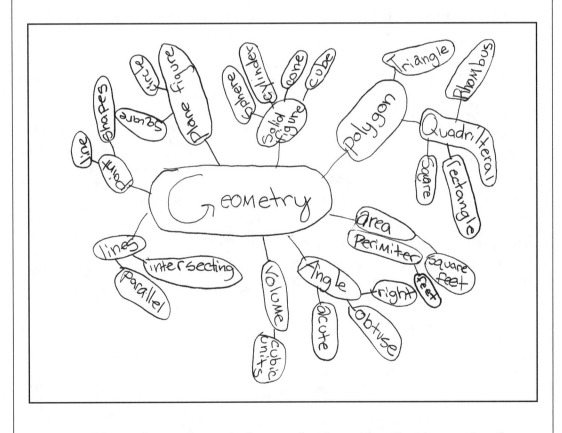

FIGURE 6.3   Creating this word web prompted students to share ideas about a variety of geometry concepts.

CLASSROOM IDEAS (continued)
Quick and Easy Vocabulary Activities

FIGURE 6.4   Having students work in groups allows them to share ideas and generate many words.

justify why that word does not fit into their current groupings.)

For a sort and label activity, students were given the following words.

yard	quart	feet	ounce
inch	scale	ruler	measuring cup
pint	degree	mile	thermometer
cup	pound	gallon	ton

In this possible grouping, the students sorted the words into various types of measurement and included a category for measurement tools.

Capacity	Length	Temperature	Weight	Tools
pint	yard	degree	pound	scale
cup	inch		ton	ruler
quart	feet			measuring cup
gallon	mile			thermometer
ounce				

In the next grouping, students placed the measurement tools within the category to which they were related (e.g., thermometer measures temperature).

Capacity	Length	Temperature	Weight
pint	yard	degree	pound
cup	inch	thermometer	ton
quart	feet		scale
gallon	mile		
ounce	ruler		
measuring cup			

In this grouping, students recognized the broader categories of measurement tools and units.

Units of Measurement	Measurement Mea-Tools
pint	measuring cup
cup	ruler
quart	thermometer
gallon	scale
ounce	

CLASSROOM IDEAS (continued)
Quick and Easy Vocabulary Activities

Units of Measurement
yard
inch
feet
mile
degree
pound
ton

Measurement Tools

Variation: For a hands-on version, math words can be placed on cards and students asked to sort them into groups and to explain their groupings. This variation provides students with a physical way to explore the words and their meanings. For primary students, words might include: *nickel, dime, hour, minute, quarter, penny, clock, second.* Do any words belong in both groups (e.g., does

quarter relate to time and money)? Don't miss any opportunities to talk about word meanings!

Word Boxes
Students are given a math word and a word box (see sample in Appendix F) and are to complete each box for the highlighted word (see Figure 6.5). The sections of the box might ask students to define, describe, illustrate, provide real-world examples, write word problems, or list related words. Word boxes can be displayed on bulletin boards or compiled into individual or class books.

Variation: Rather than using the word box template, have students fold a piece of paper into four sections and tell them (or indicate with a template on the board) what should be recorded in each section. If time

---

Word Box

My definition: An equal chance of getting of somthing or not getting something.	A real world use: To decide who gets the ball first in a football game they flip a coin and each team has an eaqually likely chance of getting their side of the coin

equally likely

An illustration: (Matt Zak)	Other related words: probability, chance, 50/50

FIGURE 6.5 This intermediate student is able to demonstrate a clear understanding of the concept of *equally likely* through his word box responses.

CLASSROOM IDEAS (continued)
Quick and Easy Vocabulary Activities

is limited, have students fold their papers in two or three sections and select just two or three ways (e.g., define, illustrate, list related words) for the students to show their understanding of the word.

Riddles

Writing riddles is a great way to focus on word meanings. The teacher can first create riddles to solve and then ask students to work with partners to write math riddles of their own. The following are a couple riddles students created.

> I am a coin.
> I am worth 10 cents.
> I am silver.
> What am I?
>
> —DIME

> I am a fraction.
> My numerator is greater than my
>   denominator.
> My value is greater than or equal to 1.
> What am I?
>
> —IMPROPER FRACTION

Words That Go Together

The teacher provides a list of words (or words on cards displayed on a board or magnetic board) and asks a student to select any two words that go together and describe the connection (e.g., *penny* and *dime* are both coins, *penny* and *clock* are both round). The words are then replaced on the board and another student is asked to find two different words that are connected in some way and to explain the connection.

Variation: Do not replace the words. Have students keep going until they cannot find any more connected words from the remaining words on the list or board.

Analogies

Simple analogies challenge students to test their thinking. Posing some analogies and then asking them to discuss their answers with a partner will give students opportunities to talk about the connections between words and the subtleties of word meanings.

- Addition is to sum as subtraction is to
  _____.
- Five is to pentagon as _____ is to octagon.
- Inch is to mile as _____ is to kilometer.
- Degree is to temperature as pound is to
  _____.

Bingo

Vocabulary bingo is a fun way to reinforce word meanings. The teacher provides students with a list of math words and students write a word in each box on the grid. Students can select where to record each word so that each student then has a unique bingo card (see Appendix G for a variety of blank bingo grids). Teachers should select the size grid based on the students' grade level (e.g., limit number of words for primary students), the amount of time available to play the game (e.g., for short periods of time, choose the 3 × 3 grid), and the complexity of the words (e.g., when using new and complex words, choose the 3 × 3 grid; when using easier or review words, choose the 5 × 5 grid). Once students have recorded the words, the teacher calls out a definition, clue, example, or shows an illustration to match one of the words; students must then find and cover the appropriate word on their bingo cards. The winner must report the words she or he selected to match each of the clues given.

CLASSROOM IDEAS (continued)
Quick and Easy Vocabulary Activities

Label the Room

Many measurement and geometry terms can be brought to life by labeling items in the classroom; students can be asked to search for examples to illustrate specific words. The teacher can create labels on sentence strips and tape them around the room as students find appropriate examples (see Figure 6.6). Teachers might label the globe a *sphere* or the television a *rectangular prism*. The chalkboard's corner might form a *right angle* and the blind slats might be *parallel lines*. Visual clues will help students remember math terms.

FIGURE 6.6 This student helps to label the room by recognizing a *right angle*.

Summary

Understanding the meaning of words within a content area is critical to learning that content. Language plays a vital role in the development of students' conceptual understanding of mathematics and provides them with a mechanism to express their reasoning, explore problems, and communicate about math content. Vocabulary development must be integrated into math instruction for students to understand and use the words and symbols of mathematics appropriately as they process information and communicate about mathematical concepts. Through specific attention to developing students' math vocabularies, teachers strengthen their understanding of content and provide them with a critical tool for communicating about that content.

Questions for Reflection

1. What is the relationship between vocabulary development and students' ability to communicate their mathematical thinking?

2. How can math vocabulary be developed in meaningful ways?

3. Which vocabulary development activities from other content areas might be used in the math classroom?

4. Does attention to vocabulary development take time away from the teaching of math concepts? Why or why not?

💿 *On the CD-ROM*

Appendix B—Activities to Review Basic Math Facts and Computation Skills
Appendix E—Math Vocabulary Lists
Appendix F—Word Boxes
Appendix G—Bingo Cards
Appendix H—Math Writing Tasks

Suggested Resources

Griffiths, Rachel, and Margaret Clyne. 1994. *Language in the Mathematics Classroom.* Portsmouth, NH: Heinemann.

Marzano, Robert J., Debra J. Pickering, and Jane E. Pollock. 2001. *Classroom Instruction That Works: Research-Based Strategies for Increasing Student Achievement.* Alexandria, VA: Association for Supervision and Curriculum Development.

Moore, David W., Sharon Arthur Moore, Patricia M. Cunningham, and James W. Cunningham. 1994. *Developing Readers and Writers in the Content Areas, K–12.* White Plains, NY: Longman.

Murray, Miki. 2004. *Teaching Mathematics Vocabulary in Context.* Portsmouth, NH: Heinemann.

Staff Development Training Videos

Using Vocabulary and Writing Strategies to Enhance Math Learning, Grades 1 and 2. 2005. Bellevue, WA: Bureau of Education and Research.

Using Writing to Strengthen Your Students' Understanding of Math Concepts and Skills, Grades 3–6. 2005. Bellevue, WA: Bureau of Education and Research.

CHAPTER SEVEN

Students Talking to Students—The Role of Cooperative Learning

This chapter explores formal cooperative learning structures, as well as informal group or partner activities. Formal structures are those in which students have assigned roles and work together to complete a task. Such tasks can take one class period or several class periods and contain the defining elements of cooperative learning identified by Johnson and Johnson (1999), including the following.

▌ *Positive interdependence*—Students work together to achieve a common goal and fail or succeed together.

▌ *Individual accountability*—Each student must contribute and each student should learn from the experience.

▌ *Face-to-face promotive interaction*—Students assist and encourage each other.

▌ *Interpersonal and group skills*—Communication, decision-making, and conflict resolution skills are developed as students work to complete group tasks.

▌ *Group processing*—Group members reflect on how the group functioned.

Informal group activities are also discussed in this chapter because of the ease with which they can be implemented during math lessons.

For less formal group or partner activities, students work together to share ideas, predict solutions, check each other's thinking, or bring closure to a lesson. Activities can be short in duration (e.g., less than one class period) and either planned or spontaneous. Whether cooperative learning activities are formal structures or informal sharing sessions, they promote opportunities for students' active learning and reflection.

Why Engage Students in Cooperative Work?

Research on cooperative learning has shown it to be a tremendously effective method of instruction; it improves student achievement, aids in the retention of information, improves motivation, and enhances interpersonal skills (Johnson and Johnson 1999). Cooperative learning is *active* learning during which students explore, investigate, and communicate. They build understanding by working collaboratively, listening to others' ideas, building on each others' thoughts, and discussing insights and observations. Such collaborative student investigations, discussions, and reflections lead to a better understanding of content.

Group activities allow students to process information and provide them with valuable experience in communicating their ideas. The process of working together toward a common goal helps students develop strong interpersonal skills; they learn how to both lead and work with each other. They are able to experience debates over strategies and solutions, as well as reach compromise or consensus. Through cooperative learning activities, students become actively engaged in their own learning, strengthen their understanding of content, and enhance their interpersonal and communication skills (Artzt and Newman 1990).

Organizing students in cooperative groups allows them to build on each other's strengths. Some students have an aptitude for calculations, while others easily employ reasoning skills; some excel at spatial relationships and others are more analytical. Putting students together provides them with a variety of skills and tools as they attempt to solve problems and make sense of math. They share strengths and develop skills in their areas of weakness. Marzano, Pickering, and Pollock (2001) synthesized research studies and concluded that organizing students in cooperative groups has a powerful effect on learning. The National Council of Teachers of Mathematics suggests that students should have opportunities to work together to support "the development of discourse and community. Working in groups, students gradually internalize the discourse that occurs, challenging themselves by asking for reasons and, in general, accounting for their own mental work" (1991, 152).

What Is the Teacher's Role During Cooperative Learning?

The teacher's role becomes that of architect and facilitator. Prior to any cooperative learning activities, the teacher determines the groupings, plans the activity, and ensures that all necessary materials are on hand. In addition, she or he sets expectations for student involvement and behavior and provides clear and specific directions. During the task, the teacher moves throughout the room to monitor group progress and to step in when needed. After the activity, the teacher provides group feedback, as well as group and individual assessment, and provides opportunities for students to reflect on each group's process. In cooperative learning, teachers and students work together to share the responsibility of learning.

How Should Learning Groups Be Formed?

Research suggests that the formation of mixed-ability groups enhances student learning in addition to encouraging social interaction and promoting equity. Homogeneous (i.e., ability-based) groups have been shown to have little long-term benefits for high-ability students and have been shown to have a negative impact on the achievement of low-ability and average students (Marzano, Pickering, and Pollack 2001). While mixed-ability groups work well most of the time, homogeneous groups may be indicated at times to allow opportunities for differentiation.

For most elementary-level tasks, two to four students is a reasonable group size; however, the size of the group should correlate with the task you have assigned. Are you grouping students so that they have a brief opportunity to share ideas prior to starting a problem-solving task? If so, then partner-sharing would meet your needs. With larger groups (i.e., four to six students), more ideas will be shared and more hands are available to help get the job done. Large groups, however, require students to use more social skills as they attempt to hear a variety of ideas, get their ideas heard, and work toward group solutions. The shy student may be able to be uninvolved in a large group; while in partner work, it is difficult for a student to disengage from the discussion. In triads, one student may be left out because the others pair up; however, activities with three specific roles can make triads quite effective. When determining group size, consider the advantages and disadvantages of each grouping and select the one that best fits the assigned task.

How Can Cooperative Learning Be Implemented Effectively?

Many teachers shy away from cooperative learning because of concern about managing student behavior. Once student movement and talk are added into a lesson, the fear is that behavior will become difficult to control. Preplanning and clear expectations for student behavior are critical to the success of group activities. Early in the year, teachers should outline general expectations for behavior during cooperative learning activities, including movement, voice level, participation, and cooperation. Many teachers determine general rules for group work within their classrooms; post the rules so that students can refer to them during tasks; and using the rules as guidelines, reflect on the success of the groups' work following the tasks. General rules might include the following.

Listen to others
Everyone contributes
Don't interrupt
Be ready to share

The physical setting of the classroom can promote success or provide obstacles to effective cooperative learning activities. Is your room conducive to cooperative learning? Many teachers prefer to seat students at tables (i.e., clusters of desks facing each other) to make the transition from whole-class to cooperative activities easier because chairs and desks do not need to be moved to begin small-group work. Desk assignments can be changed periodically throughout the year so that students have opportunities to work with a variety of students. Identifying *partners* as those students seated next to or across from each other at the beginning of a term allows teachers to pose partner questions without stopping to assign partners at the onset of each task. If desks are in rows, it is important to

determine how they will be moved when small-group work begins so that the transition is smooth and quick.

Prior to a specific task, it is important that the teacher provide clear and specific directions. Many teachers find it helpful to state, as well as write, directions on the board for reference during the activity. Checking for understanding of the directions might include teachers asking a student to explain the task or having students turn to partners and explain the task. The goal is for students to be able to get started right away when group time begins, without having to clarify directions with another student or with the teacher. Teachers also should establish a time limit for the task and clearly communicate it to students.

During group work, students who have questions can be asked to check with their partners or to "ask three before me," which prompts them to ask the teacher only when three group members cannot answer their questions. A zero-noise signal should be established prior to the start of group work (e.g., lights flickering, 5-4-3-2-1 countdown, hand signal). If you need to talk with the entire class, the zero-noise signal allows you to call for quiet so you can clarify the task, answer questions, or guide students in their progress. A signal for noise level might also be established to remind students to lower voices when the class becomes too noisy. Many teachers use incentives such as team certificates, team points, or posting the names of teams on a special recognition bulletin board, to reinforce their expectations for group members' behavior.

In cooperative learning, an objective is for all students to be active members of the group. Teachers might decide to assign roles to each student to ensure that all members are engaged. Depending on the task, the teacher can choose appropriate roles— Leader, Observer, Reader, Recorder (Writer), Reporter, Materials Manager, Calculator, Bookkeeper, Timer, Summarizer, Checker, Encourager (Cheerleader), or any other role that will help students accomplish the task. To promote participation from all group members, Kagan (1992) suggests a technique called "talking chips": Each student has a chip or other object (e.g., a pencil) and places it in the center of the group as he or she shares an idea. When everyone has talked (i.e., placed a chip), students retrieve the chips and the process begins again.

If students begin to stray from the topic or certain members are teaching skills incorrectly to others in the group, teachers should be comfortable with pulling up a chair and joining a group. Generally, through a series of thoughtful questions, teachers can highlight misunderstandings and/or get groups back on track. Although some groups in the class may move through a task without teacher support, others may need guidance to find their inspiration or solve the problem at hand.

How Should Cooperative Learning Activities Be Evaluated?

Cooperative learning activities can be evaluated for both product and process. In evaluating the finished product, attention should be given to the content that has been learned rather than the look of the actual product. (For example, if students were asked to create a game to help others learn about fractions, the game's content should be judged more heavily than the artwork. Although some teachers assign group grades, it is very common to assign a satisfactory or unsatisfactory grade to group projects and later to assess each student's learning through individual assignments. Does it matter who came up with the idea in the group if all members learned the concept as a result of the activity? Does it matter if the finished product is correctly done thanks to one student if the others do not understand and did not grow as a result of the task?

Teachers can assess student understanding through observations, interviews, or individual tasks. A wonderful way to gather informal assessments is by listening to students as they work in groups. A great deal can be learned about content understanding by analyzing their comments. When students say, "I don't get it" or "I don't know how I got that answer," we know that there is confusion. Students who remark "I can do this!" or "This is so easy!" are showing their confidence. You will see the recognition of alternate strategies when a student remarks, "I think it's easier if you . . ."; and will recognize insights when you hear, "I know what I did wrong. I think I get it now!"

Group processing is a routine posttask activity. Students are asked to reflect on what they did well and how they can improve—to analyze their own contributions to the group task. Did they take turns? Did everyone help? Did they praise each other? Was the task completed? Such evaluations can be done orally or in writing as a group or individually. Students can be asked to evaluate themselves or other group members; Even primary students can discuss how well they worked together.

Did you share your ideas?
Did you encourage others?
Did you listen to others?
Did you folZlow directions?
Did you stay on the topic?
Did you finish the task?

Students need guidance to learn to be productive and supportive members of a group. Reflective activities help them identify critical collaboration skills.

CLASSROOM IDEAS
Quick and Easy Cooperative Learning Activities

There are many group and partner activities to actively engage students in developing an understanding of mathematics. Consider the following ideas.

Group Projects

Team members work together to complete a project or task (see Figure 7.1). Assigning roles is a good idea for group projects to ensure that each student has an individual role in completing the group's task. The following are some suggestions for tasks.

- Create a counting book
- Create a game to review a math skill
- Develop and conduct a survey, then design a graph to show the results of the survey
- Determine a menu and the cost of food for a class party using grocery ads
- Design a presentation for the class explaining the concept of symmetry; include examples of symmetrical figures using pattern blocks

FIGURE 7.1 These students report on a project for which they had to design a sandbox and calculate the materials needed to build it.

- Write a book or manual to teach the main ideas about a math concept

Bag a Problem

Each pair receives an $8 \frac{1}{2}"\times 11"$ manila envelope with a word problem taped to the front. The pair solves the problem and places the solution in the envelope. When a pair finishes, students find another pair that is also finished and trade problems. When time is up (i.e., teacher sets a time limit), pairs open the envelopes they have in front of them, take the solutions out, and compare the strategies and solutions. Pairs may share the varied solutions with the class.

Think-Write-Pair-Share

Vary the Think-Pair-Share technique (Kagan 1992) described in Chapter 6 to include writing. Ask students to first think about your question; after a brief think time, ask students to write their answers (e.g., a list of items that might weigh one pound or a list of polygons). Next, have students combine their lists with their partners' lists. Then provide time for some whole-class sharing. Writing their own list or answer ensures that all students are engaged in the task and allows you to monitor their thinking as you move throughout the classroom. Writing makes their thinking visible! Here are a few suggestions.

- What ways could you make 15 cents?
- What did you learn about fractions today?
- What can you measure with a meter stick?
- When might you need to multiply?

CLASSROOM IDEAS (continued)
Quick and Easy Cooperative Learning Activities

Lineups

In Lineups students physically order themselves in a line based on the teacher's prompt (see Andrini 1991). Lineups can be done in small groups or with an entire class. Students can be asked to line up based on quantities such as age, height, or birth date. Having them record the number on an index card will allow others to see and discuss the correctness of the completed lineup. Primary students might be given cards with whole numbers while intermediate students might be asked to order fractions or decimals. Individual students might be given names of shapes (e.g., pentagon, hexagon, octagon) and be asked to order themselves from least to greatest number of sides or angles. Connections to real-world uses of numbers can be made through lineups that use real data. For example, students creating lineups to show the batting averages of players on their favorite baseball team, with each student holding the decimal form of the batting average of a particular player and lining up from worst to best.

Roundrobin

In Roundrobin, teams of three to six students sit in circles (see Andrini 1991, Kagan 1992). The teacher presents a prompt and students brainstorm responses one at a time, taking turns in a clockwise fashion moving around the circle. Roundrobin prompts, such as the following, should have multiple responses.

- Give an example of a space (three-dimensional) figure.
- When would you need to add more than 2 numbers (column addition)?
- Name a measurement tool.

- Name something that is about 1 foot long.
- Name a time when you would need to understand fractions.
- When would you need to calculate an average?

Roundrobin prompts that ask for real-world examples are a great way to encourage students to answer, "Why do we need to know this?" Listening to students' responses is a wonderful way to check for understanding of math concepts.

Roundtable

Roundtable is similar to Roundrobin, but rather than providing oral responses, students record their responses on one sheet of paper that is passed around the circle (see Andrini 1991, Kagan 1992). As the teacher poses a question or problem, the first team member jots down his or her response and then passes the paper and pencil to the next team member who adds a different response. The paper continues to be passed clockwise until time is up. Teams then discuss their responses and share them with the class.

Pick a Card—Study Buddies

This review strategy has students working in pairs. Questions are written on index cards that are placed on the desk with the question side up. Students pick a card, discuss the answer with their partners, and then turn the card over to reveal the answer.

Showdown

In Showdown, the teacher provides each student with a paper that has three or four questions (Kagan 1992). Everyone responds individually to the first question. As students

CLASSROOM IDEAS (*continued*)
Quick and Easy Cooperative Learning Activities

complete their response, they place their pencil in the center of the group. When all members are done, they compare answers. If all agree, it is time to celebrate (i.e., silent cheer) and move on to the next question; if group members disagree, they discuss their answers and decide on the correct answer together.

Pairs Check

For the Pairs Check technique, students work in groups of four (Kagan 1992). Partners sit next to each other, with another set of partners across from them. Student 1 does the first problem and her or his partner checks to see if it is correct. Then partner 2 does the second problem and partner 1 checks it. After two problems, the pair checks with the other pair at their table. If all four students agree, they can move on to the next two problems. Pairs Check is a great way to check warm-up problems to begin a class; the problems can be a reviewed skill. Calculations or word problems will work as well as identifying shapes, patterns, fractions, measurements, counting numbers, and so on.

Mix and Match

Students are given two sets of index cards: one with answers and one with questions, or one with words and the other with definitions, or one with equations and the other with solutions. Students work with partners to match the correct cards (e.g., *pentagon* matches "a polygon with five sides and five angles"; *15* matches "11 + 4"; *meter* matches "a unit of measurement equal to 100 centimeters").

Variation: Each student in the classroom is given a question or answer card and must find the other student in the class whose card matches. Or students can be asked to create question-and-answer cards for a topic with their partners and then mix and rematch them to review the topic.

Formations

In Formations, team members work together to form a number, shape, or angle, or to illustrate a math idea using their bodies (Andrini 1991). The following are some suggestions for tasks.

- Show the number that is two less than 8.
- Show the number that is double 5.
- Form a rectangle (or a rhombus).
- Show the concept of symmetry.
- Form vertical lines (or horizontal lines).
- Show parallel (or perpendicular) lines.
- Form a right angle.

Numbered Heads

Numbered Heads Together is a particularly effective strategy for engaging all students in the project or task (Kagan 1992). Students are grouped in teams of four and are numbered 1, 2, 3, and 4. The teacher poses a question or problem for the teams to solve. After work time, the teacher calls a number and that person must explain the answer or solution to the class. Only students with that number can respond and earn points for their team. The technique can be used as a review session in which teams coach each other to learn material. This technique promotes collaboration and peer tutoring because team members recognize that all of them must understand the solution since they do not know who will be chosen to report for their group.

Summary

Cooperative learning activities can be formal or informal, lengthy or brief, for pairs or groups, homogeneous or heterogeneous. Cooperative learning prompts students to explore ideas, clarify understandings, investigate issues, and debate solutions. Sharing ideas with others helps students better understand math, strengthens communication skills, and provides opportunities for teachers to hear and observe them doing math. Using cooperative activities requires attention to planning, management, and individual accountability.

Suggested Resources

Andrini, Beth. 1991. *Cooperative Learning and Mathematics*. Capistrano, CA: Resources for Teachers.

Artzt, Alice F., and Claire M. Newman. 1990. *How to Use Cooperative Learning in the Mathematics Class*. Reston, VA: National Council of Teachers of Mathematics.

Erickson, Tim. 1989. *Get It Together—Math Problems for Groups (Grades 4–12)*. Berkeley: Regents of the University of California.

Kagan, Spencer. 1992. *Cooperative Learning*. San Clemente, CA: Resources for Teachers.

Questions for Reflection

1. What is the impact of group work on student achievement and motivation?
2. How can you ensure individual student learning?
3. Which behavior management techniques should be considered when planning cooperative learning activities?
4. What is the value of listening to and observing students working in groups?

CHAPTER EIGHT

Writing About Mathematical Understanding

Math classes in the past were devoid of writing. The answer was all that mattered and there seemed little point in explaining, justifying, or describing. In recent years, as writing began to be introduced into math classrooms, our first response was, "Why? This is math class!" The idea that math was about facts and formulas seemed to imply that writing was not a part of the discipline's study. This is not necessarily unique to mathematics; other disciplines have also evolved in the use of writing as a key instructional tool. Consider the history class in which students were asked to memorize all of the dates and battles of the American Revolution versus the class in which students discuss the reasons for and impact of the war. Consider the science class in which students were asked to memorize the periodic table versus the class in which they conduct experiments to understand the characteristics of solutions.

Independent facts are important only when there is an understanding of the underlying concepts. In which class would you rather be the student? Which class will yield more productive learning? Answers alone are not enough in today's math classrooms. We recognize that the *thinking about* those answers is equally important. The emphasis on thinking about mathematics opened the door to writing as a powerful instructional tool and assessment strategy, which this chapter explores in detail.

Why Write in Math Class?

Writing is how thoughts and understandings are conveyed to others whether explaining an idea, answering questions, sharing feelings, or convincing someone of a point of view. Writing pushes students to think in depth about ideas and to connect what they are learning to what they already know (Krpan 2001). Through writing, students reflect on their own learning—they are actively engaged in the thinking process (Moore et al. 1994). They write, refine, and organize ideas, blending their ideas with ideas they hear or read about. That formal record of their thinking can be revisited, revised, modified, and strengthened as students build on their understanding about the topic. Writing, then, is a critical tool for learning. As I sat to begin writing this chapter about a topic that I had addressed countless times, the process of pulling my ideas together into an organized, written product forced me to stop and reflect on those ideas, to organize them, to decide which were more important than others, and to find just the right words to explain the ideas to you.

Putting thoughts into writing makes thoughts visible to others. Writing has often been referred to as a window into the mind (Whitin and Whitin 2000). As teachers, this look into their thinking allows us to determine the level to which students understand math concepts. This informs decisions about what to teach next, how best to present ideas, when to revisit skills or concepts, and when to challenge students with more sophisticated thinking. When moving from a focus on the correct answer to a focus on understanding math skills and concepts, it is critical for teachers to see beyond the answer; they must see what students were thinking as they arrived at that answer. Writing stops us from making quick judgments about their knowledge and abilities and allows for an in-depth look at students' understandings.

Which Types of Writing Fit with Math Content?

We write for a variety of purposes and in a variety of forms. Describing patterns, defining terms, explaining processes, and justifying solutions are some of the writing tasks frequently done in today's math classrooms. The format students use and the information they choose to include differ depending on the writing task. If we are writing to explain how to do something, we include clear, sequenced steps. If we are writing to persuade or justify, we include supporting details. If we are writing to describe, we include a variety of descriptive words or examples. If we are defining, we invoke specific vocabulary to clearly express our meaning. In math class, it is important to provide students with opportunities to write about mathematics in a variety of ways and to offer support so that students can see effective ways to express math content.

As writing is introduced into the classroom, it is important for it to fit with the math content and lesson objectives. Writing

should flow with the math lesson and help the teacher achieve its goals. If the lesson focuses on a procedure, then an explanation of that procedure might fit well. If students are learning about geometric shapes, then descriptions might be a good way to check their understanding. If they are working on calculations, then writing word problems that relate to those calculations might be a way to connect obtaining the answer to an understanding of the process. If the lesson introduces new measurement terms, then some comparison of terms might help solidify understanding. If the lesson poses a problem and challenges students to solve it, then justification of solutions might help students bring closure to their explorations.

Writing should be a part of mathematics lessons when it can support your students' math learning or help you assess your students' understanding of the math being taught. Descriptions of some types of writing that fit well in the math classroom follow. For a variety of sample writing prompts, see Appendix H.

Math content can be conveyed and/or clarified through *pictures and diagrams*. Teachers might begin by asking students to show what they know through pictures with labels, then assist them in combining text and diagrams to better explain their mathematical ideas. Primary students might be asked to draw more than 3 kites and write the number to show how many are in their pictures. Intermediate students might be asked to illustrate the concepts of area and perimeter. A great deal of meaning can be conveyed through labeled pictures and diagrams.

Providing examples is a powerful way to communicate understanding. The use of examples in math will help many students more clearly communicate their ideas. Primary students might be asked to make a list of things that come in pairs to show their understanding of the concept. Intermediate students might be asked to give examples of events in their lives that they consider certain, impossible, likely, unlikely, and equally likely; their examples will supply information about their understanding of these concepts. For young students, examples may be the only way they can express their ideas—for example, "A sphere is like a ball." As their communication skills develop, however, examples become a way to enhance their writing—for example, "A sphere is a three-dimensional figure in geometry." "A globe and a basketball are both spheres."

Writing word problems provides a critical link between doing math (computational skills) and understanding math (conceptual knowledge). Student-created problems help teachers assess students' understanding of concepts and provide a strong foundation for math problem solving. Students might be asked to write a story problem to go with a picture or number sentence (see Figure 8.1). The goal is for students to be able to both compute the answer and understand the concept.

Writing predictions provides practice in building number sense, supports the development of sound problem-solving skills, and tests reasoning skills as students justify their predictions or estimates. Primary students might be asked to predict how many paper clips will fit from one end of their desks to the other and to explain that prediction. Intermediate students might be asked to estimate how many cubes will fit in a container and to explain how they arrived at their estimate. Predictions focus students' attention on the thinking part of the task and provide them

with data to check the reasonableness of their answers.

Definitions and descriptions allow students to show what they know about math terms and concepts. Definitions may be brief, while descriptions often include examples, illustrations, or more detail (see Figure 8.2). Primary students might be asked to describe a triangle or a color pattern they have created. Intermediate students might be asked to define an improper fraction or describe a rectangular prism. Definitions and descriptions allow teachers to see the degree to which students understand a concept.

Written explanations ask students to explain or give directions for doing a math process or solving a math problem. In this type of writing, students are asked to indicate the steps and sequence for doing that process. Primary students might be asked to explain how they figured out the number of sunny,

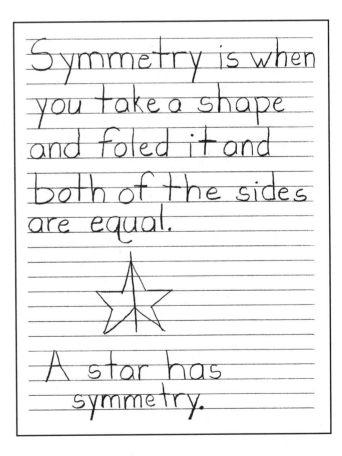

FIGURE 8.2 This second-grade student describes the concept of symmetry including an illustration and an example.

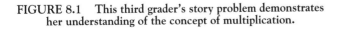

FIGURE 8.1 This third grader's story problem demonstrates her understanding of the concept of multiplication.

cloudy, and rainy days this month by looking at a classroom graph. Intermediate students might be asked to explain how to add fractions with unlike denominators or how to solve a word problem. Procedures are an important part of mathematics. Asking students to explain how they did a problem helps them think through the process they used and allows teachers to see how they arrived at their answers (see Figure 8.3).

Comparing and contrasting ideas helps students build better understandings of those ideas. Primary students might compare or contrast a penny and a nickel or a square and a triangle. Intermediate students might compare or contrast fractions, decimals, and percents. By looking at similarities and differences between math terms and concepts, students reinforce their understanding of the ideas.

Justifying a solution or process requires that students elaborate on *why* they believe the answer is correct or the process was reasonable. "Justification is central to mathematics, and even young children cannot learn mathematics with understanding without engaging in justification" (Carpenter, Franke, and Levi 2003, 85). Primary students might be asked to sort a variety of buttons into groups and then justify their groupings. Intermediate students might be asked which pizza is a better deal: a 12" round pizza that costs $6.50 or a 10" × 14" rectangular pizza that costs the same amount. The use of specific math data, combined with logical reasoning, strengthens student justifications; for an example, see Figure 8.4.

Writing summaries requires students to be able to pinpoint key ideas learned. Summaries are great closure activities for daily lessons or math units. Students might be asked to summarize what they learned about a specific math topic or to write three tips for someone learning about that topic. Summaries require students to reflect on what they've learned and to verbalize the key ideas.

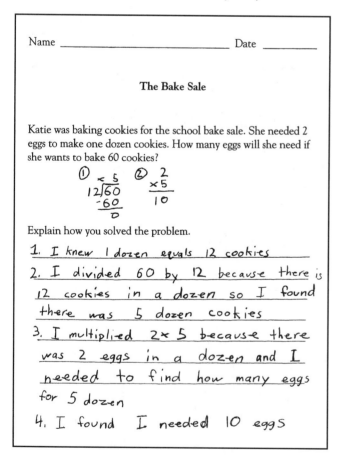

FIGURE 8.3 This intermediate student clearly explains the steps he took to solve the problem.

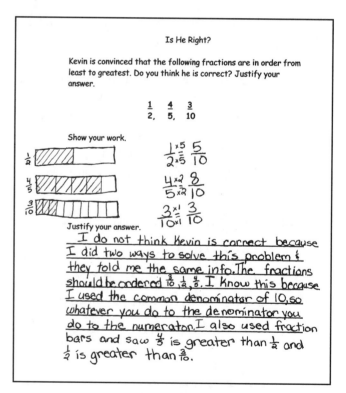

FIGURE 8.4 This fourth grader justifies her answer by using both numbers and pictures to show the needed data.

Reflective writing can focus on content knowledge, mathematical connections, or students' feelings and attitudes about learning mathematics. Reading students' reflections can provide teachers with insights into their successes, challenges, and frustrations and lead to sound instructional decisions to clarify students' misunderstandings, reteach difficult skills, connect math concepts, or support frustrated learners. Students might be asked to comment on what was difficult or easy about a particular math topic. They might be asked what they know now that they did not know last week or to list things that are still confusing to them. The comments often provide teachers with insights into how students are feeling as they learn mathematics.

Creative writing is a motivating way to blend content knowledge and language arts skills. Students can share their understanding of math concepts as they use their creativity to write stories, poems, or tall tales. Primary students might be asked to create a counting book about animals or toys or food. Intermediate students might be asked to write a story about a boy who did not understand fractions. Creative writing is a fun way to express math ideas.

Why Do Students Struggle When Writing About Math?

To effectively write about mathematics, students need knowledge of the math concepts they are attempting to express and the communication skills necessary to allow them to express their understanding. As we look at student writing, it is important to remember that those who struggle with writing about math may struggle because of a lack of understanding of content, difficulty putting thoughts into words, underdeveloped written language skills, or a combination of any of these. How to support students will differ depending on why they struggle with writing about math.

Clear writing about a concept requires a clear understanding of that concept. As Albert Einstein said: "If you can't explain it simply, you don't understand it well enough." To communicate clearly about a topic, students need to clearly understand it. Can a second grader explain how she got a subtraction answer if she does not understand the concept of subtraction? If a fourth grader does not understand how fractions are reduced to lowest terms, it is unrealistic to think that he can write an explanation of the process. In either case it is not students' writing skills that hold them back but their understanding of the content. Rather than assistance with writing skills, some students need to revisit the math concepts; once ideas are clarified, they should be better able to explain their thinking.

Other students can "do" math but may not be able to verbalize what they do. These students need help finding words to say what just happened in their heads. Gifted students may arrive at an answer quickly but are sometimes unable to explain how they got that answer. When asked how they got the answer, you might hear, "I don't know, but I know 24 is the answer." For some students, efforts to improve their abilities to write in math lead back to reflections about our instructional techniques. Can students communicate about something they don't understand? Have they heard us talk about the concepts? Will more discussions in the classroom help students increase both their conceptual understanding and their ability to express that understanding? Do they know the words (vocabulary) to say what is in their heads? The foundation for good writing about math is good thinking about math.

Clear and organized writing about a concept also requires the integration of many language arts skills such as organizing ideas, choosing appropriate words, and including all necessary information. Do students understand the question being asked? Do they know how to apply the writing skills they have learned in language arts lessons? Can they list the steps of how they did a process when asked? Do they include supporting data to justify their decisions when necessary? Are they thorough when asked to describe? Can they cite examples when asked to compare and contrast? Writing in math requires students to apply writing skills to sophisticated concepts—a challenge, but one worth posing to students.

How Can Teachers Support Students' Math Writing?

In all content areas, students often complain that writing is too difficult or that they don't like to write as they struggle to move beyond short verbal answers and put their thinking into words. It is simpler to say the answer than to write it. It is easier to provide a number answer than to have to back up the answer with reasoning and examples. We are clearly challenging students when we ask them to write about their thinking; it is more difficult than just giving answers! Offer support to students by recognizing and addressing their difficulties, by strengthening their math and writing skills, and by nurturing positive attitudes toward writing in math class.

Acknowledging the difficulty of writing about math and helping students understand the role of writing in math class will help create buy-in from those who are reluctant to write. Acknowledge that writing is not easy and that writing does take more effort than saying an answer. Praise students for their efforts at developing their writing skills even when it takes repeated effort to improve. When asked "Why do I have to write in math class?" answer honestly and fully. Let students know that their writing allows you to see their thinking and helps you better plan lessons. Let them know that you also struggle as you write but that it helps you sort out your thinking, organize your ideas, and see what you know. Assure them that you will support them as they learn to write effectively by sharing strategies, helping them find the right words as they develop vocabulary, modeling better ways for expressing ideas, and providing them with specific feedback to improve their work.

We often think of writing as an independent activity for which students receive little or no support; however, learning to write about any content requires varying levels of teacher support. Cooper (2000) suggests that independent writing is just one of a number of modes of writing (e.g., write-alouds, shared writing, guided writing, collaborative writing, independent writing), each having a different level of teacher support. Using Cooper's writing modes model allows us to see ways to scaffold support depending on the needs of students. For *write-alouds*, the mode requiring the highest level of teacher support, the teacher talks as she writes a composition or conducts a revision for the class to see. Teachers or students might write group stories during *shared writing* experiences (see Figure 8.5)—the next level

FIGURE 8.5   This primary teacher writes down students' ideas as they discuss fractions.

of support. For *guided writing*, the teacher supports students with questions and prompts as they engage in writing. This mode allows students to practice with support from the teacher. Through teacher prompting, such as asking students to orally tell them what they are thinking, teachers guide students as they write. *Collaborative writing* is when students write with a partner or group to create a single product, sharing ideas and supporting one another in the process. This mode offers peer support as students use both oral and written communication skills. For *independent writing*, students write with little or no teacher support and are able to demonstrate their own abilities.

Teachers should choose the writing mode based on the level of support that students need at a given time or for a given writing prompt. The various modes also allow teachers to differentiate their level of support based on individual student needs. For example, while the majority of the class is engaged in collaborative writing, a teacher might pull some students into a small group to do write-alouds or shared writing in order to specifically model ways to write about math.

For students who have difficulty getting their thoughts into words, teacher questioning becomes a key instructional strategy. Through scaffolded questions, teachers can pull understanding and words from students and help them learn how to put ideas into words. Modeling their own thinking through think-aloud techniques also helps students hear ideas being expressed. Partner and group work certainly allows students to hear others' verbalizations, as well as try their own ways of expressing math ideas. As students hear and verbalize ideas, they are becoming more comfortable with ways to "express" mathematics. Beginning with talk in the math classroom will allow students to generate ideas, clarify math thinking, and share ideas with others; then, they can make the ideas their own through writing.

How Can Teachers Support Writers with Various Skill Levels as They Write About Math?

Primary students, English language learners, or below-grade-level readers will need extra support to express their understanding in writing. A focus on vocabulary will greatly assist such students. Along with classroom vocabulary activities, display words on classroom walls; encourage students to keep a vocabulary log; and prior to starting the writing task, ask students to brainstorm key words that may be used in their responses.

Offering opportunities for verbalizing ideas prior to writing will be critical for students who struggle to find words to express their thoughts. Starting writing tasks with the entire class is a way to assist these students. Rather than simply asking students to get started on their written task, consider reading the activity prompt and providing a few minutes for students to discuss ideas with a partner or as a whole class. Allowing students to work with partners also can provide much-needed support.

It is important to help students develop a variety of ways to express their ideas. Will a picture or diagram help demonstrate what they know about *more than* or *multiplication* or *finding a perimeter*? Could they show that they understand *1 pound* or *congruent and similar* through an example? Can they combine text with diagrams or representations to better describe what is in their heads? Allow students to use combinations of words, pictures, and numbers to express their ideas.

Struggling students often have difficulty getting started on writing tasks. Providing a sentence starter (e.g., "I solved this problem by . . .") or using a cloze technique (e.g., "The answer is ____; I know this is the correct answer because ____.") can jump-start students and provide them with a structure into which they can insert their ideas. Frequent monitoring of their work allows you to offer suggestions, prompt thinking, and provide needed encouragement as they work to get ideas into writing.

How Should Writing Be Scored?

Every piece of writing done in the math classroom does *not* need to be scored. Some writing is simply done to practice and improve students' writing skills and/or math understanding. Rather than individually scoring *all* written work, students can share their writing with a partner or discuss their responses in a group. Teachers can facilitate a whole-class discussion following a writing task and brainstorm key ideas that could have been in students' writing as they reflect on the content and quality of their own work. Collecting and scoring student writing should be done frequently enough to evaluate student progress and obtain scores for student accountability purposes (e.g., grades and report cards).

When scoring student writing in mathematics, focus on math content and the ability to clearly express that content. Scoring rubrics help teachers evaluate the level of student responses, and inform students regarding teachers' expectations. Unlike percentages, which provide just a pinpoint score of exactly how many right or wrong answers were given, rubrics measure open-ended thinking and give more of a ballpark score. Open-ended responses can rarely be marked right or wrong, but often reveal a degree of rightness mixed with a degree of wrongness.

Rubrics allow us to sort student work into categories relative to the level of their understanding from "didn't get it at all" to "could teach the class about this concept." DeBolt (1998) warns that teachers should not make scoring so laborious that it limits the amount of writing they assign to students because it is through ongoing writing experiences that students improve their learning. For some generic rubrics for scoring math writing, see Appendix I.

Should Math Writing Be Scored for Language Mechanics?

In deciding how to evaluate students' writing about math, it is important to determine whether students were asked to do a piece of writing to be *published* or a brief constructed response. For published writing, students are allowed to edit, proofread, and rewrite. It alerts students that it is to be a polished piece of work that will be scored for writing conventions such as spelling, grammar, capitalization, and punctuation. In mathematics, published writing is generally reserved for projects, research papers, or writing activities that are combined math/language arts tasks—for example: "Write a letter to the cereal company to persuade them to use the data you collected on cereal likes and dislikes to create their newest product." Writing tasks that allow students time to move through the steps of the writing process (i.e., prewrite, rough draft, edit, proofread, publish), and that alert them that their writing should be in published form, can be scored for both content and language mechanics.

Most writing in mathematics, however, asks for brief constructed responses—short answers to show an understanding of the mathematics. Prompts direct students to clearly, thoroughly, accurately, but briefly, answer a question related to their math understanding. The purpose of this type of writing is to communicate ideas, so it is scored for the math ideas' correctness and for students' ability to clearly, thoroughly, and accurately communicate their ideas. That is not to say that students should not always be encouraged to use proper mechanics, because the purpose for using accurate mechanics is to make writing clear and easy to understand. However, communicating about difficult content, and having to apply a variety of language arts skills while doing it, is a complex task. Allowing students to focus on expressing content will provide them with important practice in expressing math ideas. Much the same as supporting students with calculators during problem-solving instruction so that they can focus on the difficult skills involved in problem solving, students should focus on the expression of ideas during writing in math. Focusing on every mechanical error can take the emphasis away from content understanding. Students' willingness to use correct vocabulary will be minimal if they are "scored down" for each misspelled word. Although we should always strive for students to apply their language arts skills to writing in any content area, writing in math class generally is not scored for language mechanics.

Which Types of Feedback Help Students Improve Writing Quality?

Students struggle with the ability to clearly and thoroughly write about math ideas. As mentioned before, student discussions and teacher modeling are important in strengthening students' mathematical thinking and ability to verbalize that thinking. In addition, students need frequent and specific feedback to help them understand the expectations for their writing and to help them refine, clarify, and improve its quality. Teachers can provide feedback to students in a variety of ways, including individual feedback through rubric scoring. While individual feedback is critical because it provides students with specific scoring and comments based on their pieces of work, there are also ways in which teachers can provide feedback to all students through whole-class discussions and activities that help them understand how to improve their writing.

At times, teachers may decide that students need to see writing in progress. Ask students to put their pencils down and then model writing on chart paper, the board, or an overhead projector. You can ask students to provide ideas for what should be in a written response as you use think-aloud techniques while students observe and assist.

Critiquing writing is a wonderful way to help students focus on what makes a good response. Following a writing activity, find a few student samples that have some good points but could also be improved. Make overhead transparencies of those pieces of work, without students' names, and use them for a whole-class discussion. Ask students the following two questions about the work samples.

1. What did this student do well?—Allow time for students to share specific ideas such as "She added correctly." "She wrote all of the steps." "She put in a diagram to show us how she did it."
2. How could this writing be improved?— Again, ask for student responses. Students might comment: "She didn't tell us why she did it." "She forgot to explain what she did." "She could have given an example so we would understand it better." With a marker, change, clarify, or add information to improve the writing.

Critiquing work with students helps to focus them on what is good and what could be better about a piece of work. Using real student work, even at the primary level, engages students in the discussion and helps them see that it is okay not to be perfect and that all work can be improved. Learning is about finding ways to constantly improve our efforts, and students' positive responses to this activity are directly related to our positive attitudes in facilitating the discussions.

How Do Graphic Organizers Enhance Math Understanding?

Writing about mathematics is our students' way of showing what they know. At times, that writing might be lists of ideas or paragraphs to explain their thinking. The writing might be words combined with diagrams or representations that together clearly tell what a student knows. Graphic organizers are another way for students to show their understanding. They can be used as a prewriting technique to help students organize their ideas and later convert them to a more polished form, or graphic organizers can be end products that allow students to express their ideas in a diagram format. Remember, all writing does not need to be a polished, edited version. Writing can be simply a tool to help organize thoughts and better understand information.

Through a graphic organizer, a student is able to use both words and diagrams to sort ideas and express ideas. Chapter 6 discussed the use of webs to allow students to make word associations and show their understanding of math concepts. Webs are an effective graphic organizer for brainstorming, recording, and organizing associations. There are a variety of other graphic organizers to support student understanding and allow them to express that understanding in a written way; descriptions of some of them follow. (For graphic organizer templates, see Appendix J.)

Sequence chains help students identify steps in a process. The links or boxes in the chain isolate the separate steps and the arrows show the order in which the steps are to be done. Sequence chains can be helpful when asking students to explain how they do a math process or how they solve a math problem. When steps and order are critical to the writing, sequence chains make those factors visible to students and provide them with a clear structure to express them.

Venn diagrams are widely used graphic organizers in mathematics. As primary students compare and contrast a dime and a nickel, and intermediate students compare and contrast a rhombus and a trapezoid, they are able to use intertwined circles to better visualize the similarities and differences between the concepts. For younger students, consider using two different colors for the two circles. If a Venn diagram is created on a board with a red chalk circle and blue chalk circle, it is easier for young students to understand when a word or phrase is recorded in both circles because it is clearly visible in the red circle and the blue circle. As students gain skill with the diagram, consider adding items that do not belong in either circle so that they can begin to see the possibility of recording an item outside the circles. For intermediate students, consider adding a third circle to the diagram to further challenge their thinking. Students might be asked to compare circles, squares, and triangles or fractions, decimals, and percents. Venn diagrams provide a clear structure for visualizing the similarities and differences between concepts (see Figure 8.6).

KWL (i.e., What I Know/What I Want to Know/What I Learned; or What I Know/What I Wonder/What I Learned) charts are used in many areas of the curriculum. A KWL chart focuses students on a topic, prompts them to share what they already know about the topic, asks them to predict what they might need to or want to know about that topic, and allows them to list what they have learned. Such a chart can be done as a whole class, in small groups, or with partners.

The first two columns are done at the start of the unit or topic. To complete the first column, students brainstorm what they already know about the topic as the teacher or another student records their ideas. This allows them to "dust off the cobwebs" and remember what they had previously learned. It sets a context for the lessons to come, and it provides teachers with some important pre-assessment data. The second column of the chart is completed next, as students and teacher develop questions to answer during

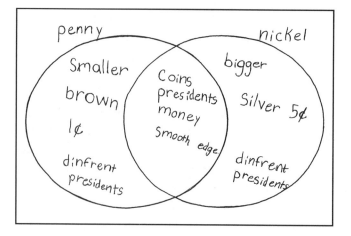

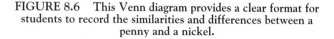

FIGURE 8.6   This Venn diagram provides a clear format for students to record the similarities and differences between a penny and a nickel.

the coming unit. In mathematics, this column of the chart can be a difficult one to complete for students who do not know what they still have to learn about a topic. Consider having students scan the upcoming chapter, directing them to look at diagrams, headings, bold print, and italicized words. The chapter scan should generate questions as students see words that they do not recognize, diagrams that alert them to a new skill, or headings that provide clues to a new concept. The first two completed columns of the KWL chart serve as a guide for exploring the unit's content. The third column provides a place to record new ideas or answers to questions either as they are discovered throughout the unit or in a summarizing lesson at the end of the unit. Used in this way, the KWL is an effective tool for linking past knowledge to current content.

CLASSROOM IDEAS
Tips for Enhancing Students' Writing About Math

Word Splash
After reading a prompt to the class, ask students to suggest some words that might appear in their written response. This can be done as a whole-class discussion or as a partner activity. Record a few appropriate vocabulary words on the board. As students construct their written responses, they can use the words "splashed" on the board. This technique helps students focus on the use of key vocabulary as they develop their responses.

Sequencing Steps to a Process
Students are frequently asked to explain how they did a math procedure; (for example: "Explain how you solved this problem." "Explain how to add fractions with unlike denominators."). Critical to this type of writing is students' ability to explain the steps of a procedure in a logical sequence. Some students respond with broad generalizations— "I multiplied"—rather than elaborating on the steps taken. Model for students how to break the process into steps. Working with the whole class or a small group, ask students to explain how they did a math process. Use sentence strips to record each separate step mentioned by students. Reread the sentence strips to the class and pose questions; for example: "Are we missing any important steps?" "Do we need to add anything?" "Do we need to change the order?" Move the strips to a more logical sequence or add other phrases for missing steps. When finished, discuss the importance of including all steps in the correct sequence.

Numbered Lists
Have students record the steps in a procedure in a numbered list format, as follows, rather than a paragraph. This format reminds students of the importance of steps and order in this type of writing and supports them in organizing and expressing their ideas about the procedure.

1.
2.
3.

First, Next, Finally
Demonstrate that numbered lists or paragraphs are both effective ways to write steps for procedures. Recipe cards that give directions for a cooking procedure are a good example of this because some are written in paragraphs and others in numbered lists. If students choose to explain math procedures

---

CLASSROOM IDEAS (continued)
Tips for Enhancing Students' Writing About Math

in paragraph form, the use of sequence words will help them maintain order and clarity. Have students brainstorm a list of words that provide clues about sequence (e.g., first, second, next, then, finally). Display sequence words on a bulletin board so that students are reminded to use them in their writing.

- First . . . Second . . . Third . . .
- First . . . Next . . Then . . . Last . . .
- To begin with . . . Finally . . .
- Additionally . . . So . . .

Convince Me!

Many times students are asked to defend or to justify their math solutions. In doing so, they must come up with supporting information, math data and/or logical reasoning to prove the correctness of their answers or of their thought processes. Justifications should convince the reader that the answer is correct or that the method is appropriate. Generally, the more specific the data, the more convincing the argument will be. Pose problems for students to solve and ask them to convince you of their answers. This can be done orally or in writing. There are tremendous benefits to doing this orally because all students are able to hear your comments as you ask for more detail or praise students' convincing arguments. The following are some prompts to use.

- What is the correct answer to this problem? Convince me!

- Which is greater: $2\frac{1}{2}$ feet or $\frac{2}{3}$ of a yard? Convince me!

- Which is greater: the number of sides on a hexagon or the number of angles on a pentagon? Convince me!

- Which is the best buy: 5 CDs for $25.00, 3 CDs for $10.00, or 10 CDs for $43.00? Convince me!

Students should use math data and/or reasoning skills to formulate an argument to convince you of their answers.

Summary

Writing is a wonderful instructional tool because it helps students organize, clarify, and make sense of their ideas, and it is an effective assessment tool because it assists teachers in seeing what students know and the degree to which they know it. Writing about mathematics pushes students to give answers and to back up those answers with reasoning and proof. It shifts the focus from answers alone to answers based on understanding.

Writing about math is challenging for many students because it requires them to understand concepts, to be able to express their ideas in words, and to apply their writing skills to produce a written product. Through writing, however, students are challenged to think about the mathematics that they do and are pushed to understand and to communicate at a higher level.

 *On the CD-ROM*

Appendix H—Math Writing Tasks
Appendix I—Rubrics
Appendix J—Graphic Organizers

Questions for Reflection

1. What are some of the challenges of getting students to write effectively about mathematics?
2. What insights have you gained from reading students' writing? How have those insights informed your instructional decision making?
3. How does the use of graphic organizers support students' development of math concepts?
4. Which types of feedback will help students improve their writing abilities?
5. Compare the roles of teaching writing for language arts teachers and math teachers. What are their common goals? How and why might their instruction differ? How can they support each other?

Suggested Resources

Burns, Marilyn. 1995. *Writing in Math Class: A Resource for Grades K–8*. Sausalito, CA: Math Solutions Publications.

Cooper, J. David. 2000. *Literacy: Helping Children Construct Meaning*. Boston: Houghton Mifflin.

DeBolt, Virginia. 1998. *Write! Mathematics*. San Clemente, CA: Kagan Cooperative Learning.

Krpan, Cathy Marks. 2001. *The Write Math: Writing in the Math Class*. Parsippany, NJ: Dale Seymour.

O'Connell, Susan R. 2001. *Math—The Write Way* (a series of three books for grades 2–3, 4–5, and 6–7). Grand Rapids, MI: Frank Schaffer Publications.

Westley, Joan. 1994. *Puddle Questions: Assessing Mathematical Thinking* (a series with a book for every grade level). Mountain View, CA: Creative Publications.

Staff Development Training Videos

Using Vocabulary and Writing Strategies to Enhance Math Learning, Grades 1 and 2. 2005. Bellevue, WA: Bureau of Education and Research.

Using Writing to Strengthen Your Students' Understanding of Math Concepts and Skills, Grades 3–6. 2005. Bellevue, WA: Bureau of Education and Research.

CHAPTER NINE

Reaching Out to All Students Through Differentiated Instruction

In the past, teachers used one dominant instructional technique (lecture combined with drill and practice) to teach mathematics, but we no longer accept that there is one way to teach math to every student. So far, the chapters of this book have explored the power of using various instructional approaches to develop skills and conceptual understanding for all students within classrooms regardless of their learning styles, readiness levels, or interests. As teachers, we are constantly challenged to find strategies that will support each student with learning, retaining, and applying math skills. This chapter focuses on ways to help all students understand mathematics by differentiating instruction.

Why Differentiate Math Instruction?

When searching for effective instructional practices for mathematics, we recognize that one size does not fit all. Instructional strategies that work for some of our students are often ineffective for others. Although students may sit in the same classroom and participate in

the same lesson, all of them do not understand at the same level or apply their learning in the same way.

A reasonable starting point for differentiating instruction is in lesson design that is attentive to a variety of student learning styles. Much has been written about the ways in which students learn information, and how our ability to reach students can be enhanced when their varied learning styles are addressed. As educators, we have focused attention on the differences between auditory, visual, and kinesthetic learners, and Howard Gardner (1993) has increased our awareness of learning preferences through his theory of multiple intelligences.

Strong, Thomas, Perini, and Silver (2004) identified four mathematics learning styles—mastery, understanding, interpersonal, and self-expressive. The styles suggest that students favor one of the following four approaches for learning mathematics: step-by-step computations, reasoning with explanations and proof, applications through group discussions and connections to real life, and visualization/exploration. Their work suggests that designing units that incorporate procedural, conceptual, contextual, and investigative styles will ensure the success of the various learners within classrooms.

What Is Differentiated Instruction?

In a differentiated classroom, varied instructional formats and techniques are evident, and student knowledge and understanding is assessed in a variety of ways. Differentiated instruction is not individualized instruction, but rather a process of changing classroom practices to provide students with various ways to acquire content, process ideas, and express their understandings (Tomlinson 2001). In a differentiated classroom, students might work individually, with partners, in groups, or in whole-class activities. They might have opportunities to explore ideas through visual, verbal, and hands-on activities. Ongoing assessment is an important component of the differentiated classroom. Preassessments are used to determine students' strengths and needs and to drive instructional planning, and a variety of continued assessments help to determine students' growth.

A differentiated classroom is a mix of whole-class, small-group, and individual activities that push each child to continue to grow in his or her math understanding. At times, all students might participate in the same lessons; at other times, the teacher might conduct a mini-workshop for a small group of students who are struggling with a skill or concept, or meet with a group of students who have mastered the skill and push them to extend their understanding through a more challenging task. Students might work at different centers or work with groups and partners on activities that fit their needs and learning styles. A differentiated classroom provides students of various needs with varied paths to gain understanding and to show what they have learned. Through differentiated instruction, we are better able to meet the needs of students whether they are struggling to acquire understanding or moving at an advanced pace.

To make differentiation work, we must begin with a new mind-set that puts students (rather than completing textbook pages) at the center of the lesson design process. By assessing what students know and considering their learning styles and readiness skills, we can effectively, and efficiently, design lessons to address students' needs.

What Are Some Guidelines for Creating a Differentiated Math Classroom?

Student Assessment—A Foundation for Differentiation

Prior to beginning a unit or teaching a skill or concept, consider a short preassessment task to determine the level at which students may already know the skill. Such assessments do not need to be lengthy or cumbersome; brief, teacher-made preassessments can provide information regarding which students have already mastered a skill and which students lack a critical foundation skill. If students can add fractions with unlike denominators prior to the lesson sequence that has been planned, will sitting through the lessons benefit them? If students are unclear about how to find a common denominator, will they be ready for the planned lessons? Assessments can be short paper-and-pencil tasks, such as five computations ranging from easy to more difficult, or may even be observations of students as they complete a task. The results of the preassessment will help you determine student groupings, possible mini-workshop lessons, or intervention or enrichment activities.

Begin with the End in Mind

Focus on math standards when planning lessons. Think about what students should be able to know and do at the end of the unit or lesson sequence, then design activities to get them there. All students may not need to do the same activities. While one group can move quickly ahead to a project that focuses on application of skills, other students can participate in cooperative groups, mini-workshops, or centers to get them where they need to be.

Both Computation and Reasoning Skills Are Critical

Many of our teachers believed that students needed to master basic computational skills before moving on to problem-solving activities. Some students practiced and practiced and practiced and still had difficulty with certain computational skills. These students spent all of their time attempting to master the basics and never explored the rich scope of mathematics. While we still agree that basics are important, we have expanded our definition of basics and have reconsidered the role of mastery. Along with computational skills, there are many basic thinking skills that students need to explore and practice in primary grades. Students need to engage in problem-solving and reasoning tasks as they develop conceptual understanding. Exploring the link between computations and reasoning can help students better understand the mathematics they are learning. Although some students may benefit from reviewing basic facts throughout the elementary years, they should also be provided with opportunities to explore real mathematics and apply concepts to problem situations.

For example, Jenny was a second grader who struggled with her addition facts. She was unable to memorize the facts despite frequent practice sessions. As her group worked with logic problems exploring button attributes with Venn diagrams, Jenny displayed her reasoning skills by assisting her group with understanding the complex sorting activity. When struggling students are given opportunities to move beyond the basics, they often surprise teachers with their abilities. All students deserve the opportunity to extend their thinking beyond "the basics."

Differentiation Implies Attention to Both Advanced and Struggling Students' Needs

Although teachers often think about modifying activities for struggling students, it is also important to consider whether lessons are meeting the needs of advanced learners within the classroom. What if students know a skill prior to a lesson? How will they benefit from hearing that lesson? If they can demonstrate an understanding of a skill, are there other activities that would enrich that understanding rather than having them participate in the same lesson as other students within the classroom? For example, Jeremy was in fourth grade. He could do and understood multiplication with two-digit factors. As he sat through numerous lessons, he became bored and frustrated. Jeremy verbalized his dislike for math and described it as "easy, but boring."

To continue to challenge students and to ensure that they do not become bored or disengaged, we must design lessons that continue to push their growth as mathematicians. While we may initially feel overwhelmed by the thought of planning different lessons for different students, a multitude of activities can be found in teacher resource books, on Internet sites, or in teacher's editions of textbooks to assist us as we strive to challenge advanced learners. Most textbooks contain many more activities than can be done within the time allotted for math instruction. Taking time to explore supplemental materials may result in finding a wealth of activities to extend a lesson for a small group of students who are ready for the challenge.

Lessons Are Taught with a Variety of Instructional Formats and Techniques

In a differentiated classroom there is an understanding that students do not all learn through the same instructional formats and techniques. While some students excel in whole-class formats, others respond to interactive opportunities offered by partner and small-group work. Some students learn best in small teacher-led groups in which they can be guided to an understanding of the concept, and others thrive in independent formats, such as centers, or even through individual contracts. While we cannot teach every child in their preferred format all of the time, we can begin by varying the formats used within the classroom to allow every student to experience some lessons in her or his preferred format.

Varying instructional techniques will also optimize success for students. Considering the varied learning styles of students, the use of concrete materials, cooperative learning activities, modeling and demonstrations, scaffolded questions, technology, writing activities, and real-world connections are all likely to provide them with many ways to see, hear, and experience mathematics.

Students Should Be Assessed in Various Ways

Just as we strive to design lessons that meet the needs of a variety of students, we need to ensure that assessment techniques allow a variety of learners to show what they know about mathematics. From paper-and-pencil tasks to observations of students' work to student interviews, we are challenged to find multiple ways to assess student skills and understanding. Although it is easier to use the same assessment (e.g., paper-and-pencil tests) for all students, it may not provide a true look at each student's strengths and weaknesses. Can advanced students show their knowledge through projects that demonstrate an extended understanding? Can students who struggle with written tasks describe their understanding in interviews? Can students with language difficulties demonstrate their knowledge as they work with manipulatives?

Listening to students and observing their work provide invaluable information about what they understand. Portfolios in which students can self-select items provide opportunities for differentiation and engage students' interests. As students in a classroom work on assigned activities, would it be possible to conduct informal interviews to ask them about their understanding? The intent is not to individually assess each child, but to be open to the possibility of assessing some students in a way that is different from the majority of the class.

How Can Flexible Groups and Mini-Workshops Enhance Math Instruction?

In elementary teaching, it has been a long-accepted practice to group students for reading instruction. Ask any elementary teacher and he will affirm that all students do not enter a specific grade at the same reading readiness level and that they should not be taught at a frustration level. It makes *no sense* to ask students to read material that is too difficult for them, and asking advanced readers to read at a lower level will not challenge them or advance their skills. When faced with designing classroom math lessons, however, it has been a common practice to teach all students at the same level. Do they come to class at the same readiness level in math? Will students who are taught at a frustration level succeed?

Grouping students definitely takes more time and effort than teaching to the whole class. It may require designing several variations of a lesson rather than one for all students. If grouping occurs, it requires thought to what others will do when we are working with a small group. Flexible grouping does present a bit more complexity to math planning, but it is more likely to meet the needs of our students and help them all progress in their understanding of mathematics.

Rather than assigning students to a group for the duration of the year, flexible grouping provides teachers with the best tool for meeting students' needs and allows us flexibility to teach through a variety of formats depending on the skills and concepts being addressed. Through flexible grouping, students move in and out of groups based on their needs and abilities. They are able to experience whole-class instruction, cooperative groups, small teacher-led groups, and individual tasks, and students have the opportunity to work with all of their peers through combinations of heterogeneous and homogeneous groupings. On one day, students may work as a whole class, the next day there may be two activities going on simultaneously, and on still another day students may be working at centers or in small teacher-led groups.

Mini-workshops—small teacher-led groups designed to teach or reteach a skill—meet as needs arise and are comprised of students who might benefit from the group lesson (see Figure 9.1). Specific students can be invited to join the mini-workshop or the teacher might invite any interested student to join. Invitations to join mini-workshops will vary depending on the concept. In mathematics, frequently a student who understands geometry may struggle with measurement skills. A student who can effectively reason through problems may have difficulty calculating a correct answer. Consider the topic or skill and give students the opportunity to move in and out of groups as necessary.

Mini-workshops are often created as teachers notice varied levels of understanding following whole-class lessons. In one fifth-grade classroom, students were working on their understanding of percentages. The

teacher decided to conduct a mini-workshop for students who needed additional support with the computation of percentages, while others who had already mastered the process searched through newspapers for examples of percentages and began developing their own problems based on what they found. Following the 15-minute mini-workshop during which the teacher re-explained the procedure as she used real examples to show the meaningfulness of the task, she assigned a few practice problems to the small group to ensure that students had understood the lesson. The teacher then turned to the remainder of the class to discuss their student-generated problems. Several of the problems were then used as a task for all students to solve and both groups discussed the problems and solutions together. Each group received the support that it needed—fair, but not equal.

Some Keys for Effectively Managing Flexible Groups

Smoothly run groups are the result of students understanding your expectations about work

FIGURE 9.1   Mini-workshops allow teachers to work with small groups of students to provide more individualized support.

completion and behavior. Students need to clearly understand what is expected of them both in and out of groups. During teacher-led groups, the teacher is visible and helps to manage behavior by his presence; however, when students are away from the group, expectations must be especially clear so that they can manage their own productivity and behavior.

Providing substantive and motivating anchor activities for students to engage in when they have finished their assigned tasks is essential. There may be several activities for students to choose from, but activity directions, expectations for the finished product, and the behavior expected as they engage in an activity should be understood by all students. Options for anchor activities include solving a problem of the week (POW) challenge, exploring patterns on 100 Charts, writing a math journal entry, or practicing math facts. Discussions about movement allowed within the classroom, which tasks should be completed and in what order, and the level of acceptable noise are critical. Anchor activi-

ties should be productive and engaging ones that will support the development of necessary skills and concepts, not simply busywork assignments.

How Can Centers Be Used to Support All Learners' Needs?

Classroom centers offer another way to differentiate instruction; they allow students to explore math skills and concepts, often in hands-on or interactive ways. Centers can be designed to provide additional practice for students having difficulty with a skill or concept, to provide opportunities for students to apply previously taught skills to a new situation, and/or to provide enrichment opportunities to challenge a student who has mastered the skill (see Figure 9.2). Depending on the size and arrangement of a classroom, centers might be a physical place within it in which materials and activities are available for student participation; for smaller classrooms, centers might be portable with materials and activities in folders, crates, or baskets that can be taken back to

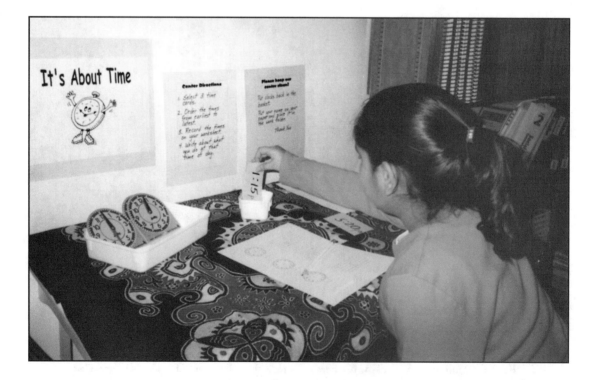

FIGURE 9.2   Through centers, teachers can address the various levels of students' needs.

FIGURE 9.3 In some classrooms, it may be necessary to create centers through the use of folders or baskets that can be brought to students' desks.

students' seats. Centers can pose individual, partner, or group tasks (see Figure 9.3).

Centers can be a regular part of math instructional time with all students rotating through them, or they can be specifically designed for a small group of students either to review a skill or provide a challenging extension. Centers can also provide engaging activities for students who are not involved in a mini-workshop or who have completed their assigned math task.

For some teachers, the idea of centers is synonymous with labor. Many remember the days of cutting out dozens of shapes and pieces to create interactive puzzles and games with self-checking answer sheets. We also remember our frustration when one piece disappeared and the activity was no longer functional, or the depression when it was time to replace the centers with new ones, each with a multitude of pieces. Centers do not have to be labor-intense to support students' math understanding.

Consider some generic math centers. Perhaps a counting center with a basket of objects to be counted. It is simple to change the objects each week. A measurement center might include a scale, a ruler, or a measuring cup and various objects for students to measure and then record the measurements. A math literature center might highlight several books and ask students to draw a picture or write a

paragraph to show the math within the book. A graphing center might have a graph of the week and prompt students to answer questions or write about what they learned from the graph. Manipulative centers might give students practice creating original patterns with pattern blocks, tangrams, or multilink cubes. Computer centers might provide opportunities for students to explore software that supports their math skills. Many other centers can be designed to help students review, refine, and extend their understanding. For a variety of math center ideas, see Appendix K.

Some Keys for Effectively Managing Centers

Appealing centers are attractive and engaging. At a center, students should be able to be successful on their own. Because students are expected to work independently, it is critical that teachers properly introduce them to the objectives, directions, and expectations for each center. Centers should be introduced one at a time. Directions should be clearly displayed in a way that students can understand (e.g., visuals may be needed for primary students), and all materials should be available. When necessary, a sample of the center product can be displayed.

A system should be in place to let students know when they may visit a center. Some teachers use pocket folders and index cards with students' names placed in the pockets for the appropriate center; others put students' names on clothespins and clip them to a poster displaying each center's name; and still others post a list and have each student alert the following student when it is her or his turn to go to the center.

During an initial orientation, it is important to discuss the following procedures for use of each center.

Who is allowed to visit the center?
How many students can be at a center at one time?
How long can a student remain at a center?
What behaviors are expected of students when at centers?

If center participation results in a finished product, where is it to be placed?

What kind of cleanup is expected?

Teachers may have a variety of answers to each of these questions. We don't need to answer them in the same way; the important thing is that we know (and students know) the answers to each of the questions. Initially having students participate in centers while observing and reinforcing the rules and procedures will result in those behaviors being likely to occur even when you are occupied with a student or group of students and are unable to monitor center behavior. Remember, the privilege of participating in centers can be revoked if a student's behavior is disruptive to the class.

How Can Assignments Be Adjusted for Various Readiness Levels?

There are a variety of ways to adjust the quantity, complexity, and time given for task completion. Tiering is a way to adjust the difficulty level of a task or assignment by providing multiple versions for various ability levels. Two versions of the same task can be prepared so that students receive the one that best matches their readiness level. A problem might be adapted by using simpler data or fewer calculations in one version.

Consider extending the time allotted to teach a skill or strategy to struggling students. Some students will benefit from additional lesson presentation time, review sessions, or participating in mini-workshops. Also consider increasing the time allowed to complete an assignment or permit students to finish an assignment for homework. For advanced learners, add a second tier to an activity so that students can extend the concept if they finish quickly.

Reduce or increase the number of computations or problems students must complete depending on their skills and abilities. You might circle the computations on a worksheet that students should complete or cross off any that do not need to be completed. Alternatively, consider cutting worksheets in half and giving the first part to all students; as they finish that half, individually give out part two. This allows for a quick scan of their work so that you can step in to support those who are off-track before they proceed to the second part of the task.

CLASSROOM IDEAS
Quick and Easy Ideas for Differentiating Instruction

There is no one *best* strategy that works for all students, but there are a variety of research-based and classroom-tested approaches that enable us to select strategies that match the varied learning styles of students. Consider the ideas in the following lists.

For Visual Learners

- Use pictures, charts, maps, and graphs whenever possible.
- Demonstrate procedures and illustrate concepts using visual demonstrations (e.g., overhead manipulatives or magnetic cutouts).

- Include diagrams when posting vocabulary words (e.g., parallel, right angle, hexagon).
- Encourage students to take notes and draw pictures or diagrams in their notes; have students highlight and underline key ideas.
- Highlight rows on a multiplication chart with strips of colored transparencies or strips cut from colored transparent report covers to focus attention to certain numbers (see Forsten, Grant, and Hollas 2002).

CLASSROOM IDEAS (*continued*)
Quick and Easy Ideas for Differentiating Instruction

- Place worksheets in page protectors and allow students to write on the plastic cover with wet-erase markers (Forsten, Grant, and Hollas 2002).
- Use graphic organizers to illustrate procedures or concepts.
- Have students illustrate word problems.
- Use a variety of media (e.g., computers, videos) in lessons.
- Share illustrated books that support math concepts.
- Emphasize illustrations and diagrams in the math text.
- Allow students to use pictures, diagrams, examples, and/or representations to show what they know.

For Auditory Learners
- Provide lots of class discussions and group work to review ideas.
- Talk through solving problems or doing procedures using a think-aloud technique.
- Allow students to show their understanding through oral presentations.
- Have students read text, problems, procedures, or solutions aloud.
- Encourage students to recite responses.
- Pair students to read and work on problems or to periodically discuss their progress with a partner.
- Have students create songs, poems, or mnemonics to aid memorization.
- Instead of answering a problem in writing, allow a verbal response from some students.
- Assign peer buddies or cross-grade level tutors to provide some extra support.
- Consider training "home partners" (parents or other relatives) to provide additional support at home.

For Tactile/Kinesthetic Learners
- Include movement whenever possible (see Classroom Ideas in Chapter 7 for lineups to sequence numbers, formations to show geometric shapes, etc.).
- Use manipulatives to provide hands-on exploration of concepts (e.g., geoboards to show geometric shapes, Unifix cubes to create patterns, pattern block designs to explore symmetry).
- Have students create interactive study guides by folding paper into sections and recording ideas in each section; for example, two-fold paper with odd and even numbers recorded; three-fold paper with acute, obtuse, and right-angle illustrations and definitions; four-fold paper with examples of problems that can be solved using addition, subtraction, multiplication, and division (see Zike 2003).
- Help students line up numbers for computations by turning loose-leaf paper on its side so that the lines form columns or by using graph paper.
- Allow students to move to centers to work on hands-on activities.
- Use physical models to show concepts (e.g., models of space figures such as cylinders and spheres, measurement tools such as thermometers to show temperature, or scales to show weight).
- Have students sort and categorize ideas using words on index cards.
- Act out story problems.
- Create physical graphs or Venn diagrams using students as examples.
- Provide interactive games using dice, spinners, cards, and so on to illustrate and practice math skills.

CLASSROOM IDEAS (*continued*)

Quick and Easy Ideas for Differentiating Instruction

- Have baskets of materials (e.g., colored chips, cubes, calculators, paper and pencils) available in the classroom and allow students to access the materials as they need them to complete tasks.
- Consider the use of standing workstations or allowing students to relocate to another section of the room to complete their work; movement may be just what they need to refocus and process information.
- Encourage all-pupil-response techniques by using pinch cards (O'Connell 2000) or individual black boards or white boards.
- Create interactive review puzzles by cutting questions and answers apart and having students match the correct answer to each question.

Summary

All students do not learn mathematics in the same way or at the same pace. Meeting the needs of the students within a math classroom requires varied instructional approaches, ongoing assessment, and attention to the various learning styles and readiness levels of students. Through differentiating instruction, teachers can design lessons to meet the needs of a variety of learners rather than designing lessons that offer a single approach to learning the mathematics content.

Suggested Resources

Forsten, Char, Jim Grant, and Betty Hollas. 2002. *Differentiated Instruction: Different Strategies for Different Learners*. Peterborough, NH: Crystal Springs Books.

Tomlinson, Carol Ann. 2001. *How to Differentiate Instruction in Mixed-Ability Classrooms, Second Edition*. Alexandria, VA: Association for Supervision and Curriculum Development.

Tomlinson, Carol Ann, and Caroline Cunningham Eidson. 2003. *Differentiation in Practice: A Resource Guide for Differentiating Curriculum*. Alexandria, VA: Association for Supervision and Curriculum Development.

Zike, Dinah. 2003. *Big Book of Math*. San Antonio: Dinah-Might Adventures, LP.

On the CD-ROM

Appendix K—Math Centers

Questions for Reflection

1. How will you identify the readiness skills of students within the classroom?
2. How will you plan for the variety of learning styles within your classroom?
3. Discuss the challenges of flexible grouping. Suggest one possible solution for each challenge you identify.
4. How can centers enhance a math classroom? What must be in place to ensure that centers are effective and manageable?
5. How will you identify students who already know the skill you are planning to teach? How will you adjust the instruction to meet their needs?

CHAPTER TEN

The Role of Technology in Enhancing Teaching and Learning

Not long ago, technology in the classroom consisted primarily of drill-and-practice software, which allowed students to practice basic computational skills. Today, technology is central to learning and teaching as an instructional tool, a communication tool, and a research and planning tool. The National Council of Teachers of Mathematics views technology as "essential in teaching and learning mathematics: it influences the mathematics that is taught and enhances students' learning" (NCTM 2000, 373).

Technology supports teachers and students in a multitude of ways. Commercial software and websites provide opportunities for students to review critical skills and/or to explore math concepts. Calculators support students as they solve problems and assist them with complex computation skills. Internet searches provide teachers with lesson planning ideas as well as access to a wide range of resources and materials for classroom lessons. Technology provides instant communication between education professionals as well as a way to provide up-to-date information to students and parents. This chapter explores the use of technology as an instructional tool, a communication tool, and a research and planning aid; and it discusses the ways that technology supports teachers and students in the elementary mathematics classroom.

What Are the Benefits of Integrating Technology into the Teaching of Elementary Mathematics?

Technology enhances student learning; using it stimulates thinking, reasoning, and problem solving (Culp, Honey, and Mandinach 2003). As students work with software, calculators, and other forms of technology, they analyze, organize, and record their thinking; and they are pushed to reflect on data, solve problems, and make decisions. In addition, the use of technology has been shown to result in more integrated and better assimilated knowledge as students work with simulations, virtual manipulation, and graphic representations that help them link new knowledge to existing ideas (Culp, Honey, and Mandinach 2003).

In their position statement on the use of technology for learning and teaching mathematics, the NCTM contends; "Students can extend the range and quality of their mathematical investigations and encounter mathematical ideas in more realistic settings" (2003). Through the support of technology, students are able to explore tasks that would otherwise be too complex for them to handle. In this way, technology opens up opportunities for many engaging, real-world scenarios in which students can explore authentic math applications.

Technology motivates and engages students. Students show greater interest and a longer attention span when technology is a part of classroom activities (Culp, Honey, and Mandinach 2003). Studies have also shown that students working in technology-rich classrooms have a more positive attitude toward learning (Apple 1995).

The role of the teacher shifts when technology is used in instruction. Learning becomes student-centered rather than teacher-centered. Teacher–student interaction is greater than in traditional classrooms because the function of the teacher changes to one of guide and facilitator (Culp, Honey, and Mandinach 2003). Students become more independent learners (Apple 1995), and teachers are better able to meet the needs of individual students through customized lessons and differentiated instruction (Hancock and Betts 1994).

Technology assists teachers in the planning and development of lessons through quick access to countless resources. Teachers are able to obtain more and varied resources and receive support in how to use those resources (Culp, Honey, and Mandinach 2003). The ability to quickly research ideas enhances student learning and streamlines teacher planning. Opportunities for teachers to interact with colleagues and share ideas about teaching and learning are readily available. Communication between teachers, students, and parents is enhanced through websites and email communications that allow for the quick-and-easy transmission of ideas.

Technology is a critical tool in today's society. Along with supporting students in the understanding and application of math skills, incorporating technology into classroom lessons helps students develop skills in using these important tools. Using technology in the classroom supports students' learning of mathematics content as well as improving their technology-use skills. (Refer to Appendix L, "Must-See" Math Websites, for more on using technology in the classroom.)

What Is the Role of Calculators in the Elementary Mathematics Classroom?

Students need to be able to calculate mentally, perform traditional paper-and-pencil computations, and use a calculator. "Calculators do not replace fluency with basic number combinations, conceptual understanding, or the ability to formulate and use efficient and accurate methods for computing. Rather, the calculator should support these goals by enhancing and stimulating learning" (NCTM 2000, 145)." Some educators have expressed concern that the use of calculators inhibits students' ability to perform basic computations; however, studies on the use of calculators suggest that they do not hinder students' abilities with basic computations if basic concepts have been developed first. Those studies also confirm that students who use calculators have a more positive attitude toward math and a better self-concept about their math abilities (Hembree and Dessart 1992).

The use of calculators stimulates thinking and supports problem solving. Calculators allow students to explore more complex tasks by assisting them with computational skills that would otherwise be difficult for them to do. Third-grade students who understand the process of addition but are unable to add large numbers can use their knowledge of the concept and their calculator skills to effectively solve problems that require such addition. Problem-solving tasks that are beyond their computational skills are suddenly doable.

Students need to employ a variety of thinking skills when using calculators because they are responsible for analyzing problem situations, inputting appropriate information, and evaluating the reasonableness of answers. Intermediate students are motivated by the use of real-world data in problem-solving activities. Using baseball statistics, menu data, or amusement park admission rates engages students in authentic problem situations that require them to demonstrate their solution skills. Supporting students with the use of calculators allows them to focus on the problem situation and their method for solving it.

Students should be encouraged to estimate answers when using the calculator. Comparing calculator answers to estimates supports the development of number sense and enhances students' thinking. Activities, such as the *Range Game* (Reys et al. 1979) and *Mystery Numbers* in the Classroom Ideas section later in this chapter, provide students with practice in mental math and support the development of number sense.

Calculators are also a wonderful way to investigate patterns and number relationships. Students can explore patterns by using the calculator's constant function and examining the results. First graders might enter [0][+][2] and then repeatedly hit the [=] key to see the calculator continue to add 2 to the previous number. Students might skip-count along as they read the computer display. Second-grade students might be asked to begin with another equation (e.g., [3][+][4][=]) and then, by repeatedly pushing the [=] key, see patterns that may be less obvious because their patterns began with the number 3 rather than 0. Students might be asked to predict the next number as the calculator adds 4 to each previous sum.

Increasing the complexity of numbers will challenge older students as they explore number patterns. Third-grade students might be asked to enter [99][−][5] and then predict

each resulting difference before pressing the [=] key. When working with older students, multiplication can be explored using the constant function; however, the first number entered will be the number that is multiplied repeatedly (e.g., [4][×][5][=] will result in each product being multiplied by 4). Students will be amazed at how rapidly the numbers become very large, quickly resulting in a number too large for the calculator to display.

Knowing how to use calculators is an important skill for the twenty-first century. The use of a specially designed overhead calculator—the keys and display can be seen when placed on a projector—allows teachers to demonstrate calculator skills in a very visual way. As students are taught to enter equations correctly, attention should be focused on how to check for the reasonableness of answers. Students should be taught to estimate answers and then compare the numbers on the calculator display to their estimated answer to determine whether the answer is reasonable.

In addition, discussions about the appropriateness and efficiency of computation methods should take place in elementary classes. Should a calculator be used when determining 3 + 2 or would mental math be more efficient? The decision to compute mentally, on paper, or with a calculator is a topic that should be discussed so that students develop an understanding of the appropriate use of the calculator as a computation tool.

Having calculators in the classroom supports students as they explore a variety of mathematical tasks, and various kinds of them are available including ones that can do tasks such as fractional computations and graphing. Teachers, however, should decide when to allow students to use calculators during classroom activities. During problem-solving tasks, calculators provide support by helping students do computations, allowing them to focus on the thinking skills. Explorations with calculators can strengthen students' number sense and understanding of operations and patterns. During activities that are to focus on the development of students' paper-and-pencil computation skills, however, elementary teachers may choose to have students practice those skills without calculator support. The objective of lessons should determine decisions about the appropriate use of instructional tools.

How Can Technology Tools Enhance the Quality of Teachers' Presentations?

Technology tools make learning more interesting. As teachers strive to present math concepts in an understandable way and to connect math ideas to students' lives, technology allows them to create attention-grabbing and motivating lessons that bring math to life. The use of overhead projectors during classroom lessons helps many students who benefit from both seeing and hearing ideas. Along with allowing teachers to display key words and symbols as they talk about math ideas, overhead projectors allow students to see demonstrations with colorful, two-dimensional overhead manipulatives. As teachers use transparent chips or pattern blocks or tangrams or fraction pieces, students are able to visualize the math ideas.

The use of video visualizers—a projection tool that projects images on a monitor or screen—allows students to view three-dimensional objects, photographs, or pages of text (see Figure 10.1). Using video visualizers, teachers can manipulate three-dimensional objects, such as multilink blocks to explore volume, while students watch the action enlarged on a screen. Samples of student work can be displayed for others to immediately see rather than having to create transparencies of work samples. A page of a textbook or children's literature book can be displayed, with sections highlighted through zoom-in technology.

Using PowerPoint, teachers can capture students' attention with colorful presentations that include graphic images, photos, and video clips. Primary students might explore

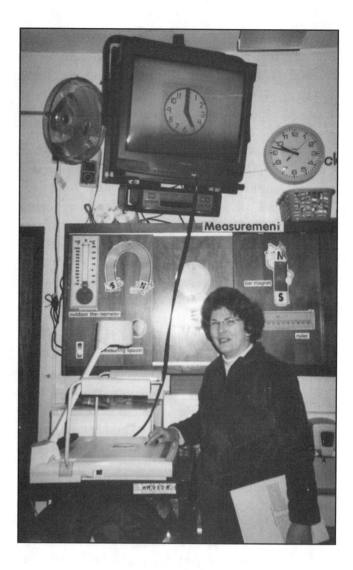

FIGURE 10.1 Visualizers allow teachers to enlarge manipulatives or student work.

three-dimensional shapes by viewing pictures of real-world objects that illustrate various space figures, while intermediate students might view perimeter through a variety of real examples as they explore photo frames or garden fences. Multimedia (LCD) projectors allow PowerPoint presentations or video clips to be projected on large screens for all students to see. Digital camera images can be easily imported into presentations, allowing teachers to insert photos of students or class projects.

Another exciting presentation tool is the SMART Board—an interactive white board. SMART Boards combine the simplicity of a white board with the power of a computer.

They have a touch-sensitive display that connects to the computer and a digital projector to show the computer image. Teachers can then control computer applications directly from the display, write notes in digital ink, and save work to share later.

Through multimedia tools, students can see and hear lessons in new and exciting ways—ways that can reach students with various learning styles. Any number of tools are available to engage students' interest and provide a variety of avenues for them to learn about mathematics.

How Can Technology Support Students as They Practice Basic Skills?

Educational software and websites are available to help students practice previously taught skills. Drill-and-practice activities are generally in game formats and can be programmed for the ability levels of students. It is recommended that students have a basic understanding of the concepts prior to engaging in computer-assisted practice. While drills that use technology probably do little more than teacher drills or partner practice, they do provide teachers with the flexibility to tailor practice to the specific skills and levels that individual students need. Plus, they can engage students in practice activities even when the teacher is unavailable for individual support. Graphics and sound often make this type of computational practice more interesting for students, and the ease of use of many of these programs makes them appropriate for classroom centers or as activities for students after they complete other assigned classroom tasks.

In selecting software or websites for drill-and-practice activities, teachers should look for ones that can be programmed to meet individual student needs. Many programs allow teachers to modify the number of problems, the complexity level of problems, or the time allotted to complete a task. Directions for engaging in the activity should be easy to understand and might include visuals to support primary students in understanding the task. Students should receive feedback for right or wrong answers, and the number of wrong answers should be limited so as not to frustrate students (e.g., after three wrong answers, students get a tutorial or clues to assist them with finding the answer). Many sites provide students with a quick assessment of their skills (e.g., the number or percentage correct) and some provide teachers with similar data. Selecting software or websites to match the needs of students is important.

Another option for skills practice is the purchase of integrated learning systems, which are computer-based instructional programs. They usually consist of curriculum materials (e.g., tutorials) for the student, an assessment system to identify student performance, and a management system that can be used to modify the course as needed for individual students. Through this type of computer-assisted instruction, teachers can print reports about student performance and students can work at their own levels. The information in these systems, however, is primarily rote instruction and repeated practice, generally with little application of skills to problem contexts.

How Can Technology Programs Promote Exploration of Concepts and Interaction with Data?

Software and websites can do more than just support students in the practice of rote skills. Students can be challenged to organize data, recognize patterns, explore concepts, solve problems, draw conclusions, and communicate their findings. Software can be purchased or teachers can access Internet-based applications (e.g., applets) to stimulate students' mathematical thinking.

Many software programs engage students in explorations and allow them to manipulate data and reason through problems. *The Graph Club* (Tom Snyder Productions) allows K–4 students to create, interpret, and print a variety of graphs—picture, bar, circle, and line—

as well as tables; and it allows students to compare different graphic representations of the same data. In the *Fizz and Martina's Math Adventures* series (Tom Snyder Productions), students in grades 1 to 6 explore problems cooperatively. The problems are linked to the computation and problem-solving skills of various grade levels and promote students' math communication skills. (The software is available at www.tomsnyder.com).

Illuminations is a website dedicated to illuminating the National Council of Teachers of Mathematics standards by providing online resources for improving the teaching and learning of mathematics (see www.illuminations.nctm.org). The website contains tools, standards, web links, and lessons to support the teaching of K–12 math. There is also a direct link to the NCTM's *Principles and Standards for School Mathematics* (2000). A significant feature of this site can be found in the *Tools* section where online, interactive, multimedia math investigations, grouped by grade level and standard, are available. The teacher versions include solutions and teacher notes. The student versions are ready for classroom use and can be used online or downloaded for use without a live Internet connection. The Illuminations website also offers a collection of lesson plans created by master teachers; the web links provided are sorted by grade level and standard.

Many websites provide electronic manipulatives through applets—Internet-based applications. Students can explore mathematics using web-based tools, such as pattern blocks, tangrams, and base-ten blocks, that are screen versions of physical manipulatives. The electronic versions often work in a more realistic way than the physical models because they can be broken apart or merged together in ways that physical manipulatives cannot (e.g., base-ten blocks can be broken into pieces rather than traded when using physical models).

Another benefit of applets is the way in which the information is displayed on the screen. When students work with physical manipulatives, they do not see the numbers and symbols that relate to the physical models. In contrast, many computer tasks display the numbers or symbols on the same screen as the electronic manipulatives—for example, as base-ten blocks are combined, the computer displays the number that coincides with the blocks on the screen. As the manipulatives are changed during the activity, the numbers on the screen change to reflect the new quantity. This provides an important bridge between pictorial and symbolic representations.

Computer explorations also have the capability of demonstrating changes in data. In some graphing software, students can enter data and then push a button to change it from a bar graph to a circle graph; or they can add or delete data to change the look of the graph. Math is a dynamic process and computers allow students to visually experience this process.

Electronic manipulatives should be easy for students to use, allow students to change and manipulate them, display a link between pictures and symbols, and focus on problem solving. Having students work in pairs encourages them to talk about their experiences as they predict, discuss, and reflect on their actions. Providing opportunities for full-class discussions about the experiences helps students reflect on their experiences and solidify their understandings.

How Do Technology Communication Tools Support Teaching and Learning?

There are a variety of communication tools that support teaching and learning. Word processors help students as they write about their mathematical thinking. Students can describe, justify, explain, and even illustrate ideas to demonstrate their math understandings. Primary students might use simple word processing software such as Kid Pix, while older students might use Hyper Studio or PowerPoint to record their ideas and share them with others (see Figure 10.2). Presenting

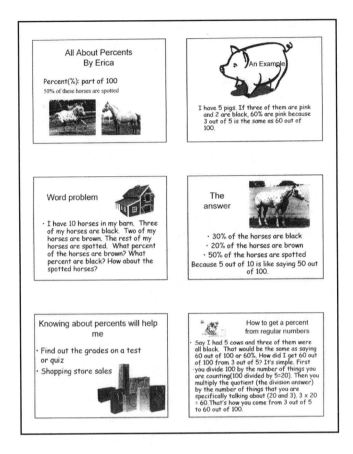

FIGURE 10.2 This intermediate student created a PowerPoint presentation to show what she knew about percents.

ideas to the class becomes easy with technology communication tools and they allow students to share information and ideas in creative ways.

Presentation software lets students share ideas with the class through multimedia presentations, which necessitates the integration of students' math ideas with their understanding of the technology. In addition, such presentations capture students' attention in a way that traditional reports do not. Primary students might insert graphics to show ideas, while intermediate students might use digital cameras to take pictures to insert into presentations. Even student-created video presentations have become common in today's elementary classrooms.

Email communication and professional websites encourage teachers to communicate with colleagues. Communicating through emails provides teachers with quick access to parents and colleagues. The websites of

professional organizations, such as the National Council of Teachers of Mathematics (www.nctm.org) or the Association of Supervision and Curriculum Development (www.ascd.org), provide teachers with an abundance of resources from professional development opportunities to classroom resources. Some websites also allow teachers to ask questions about the teaching of mathematics (e.g., the Ask Dr. Math feature at www.mathforum.org).

Websites of their own are a wonderful way for teachers to communicate with parents and students. While teachers used to create weekly or monthly newsletters to inform parents of class activities, today's teachers have found how much time and effort can be saved by using classroom websites. Even teachers with no knowledge of how to develop one can have a website through several sites (e.g., www.teacherweb.com) and can easily enter information that will then be posted on their site. Teacher websites might include daily objectives; overviews of class lessons for absent students; a record of homework and due dates; tips or help with assignments; links to the teacher's email; notices about field trips, parent conferences, or special activities; and/or links to other sites (e.g., homework help, drill-and-practice sites, problem-solving extension activities). Websites that link to a teacher's email allow for direct communication with parents and wide dissemination of information.

How Does Technology Support Teachers' Lesson Planning and Professional Development?

As teachers, we have traditionally spent most of our time in our own classrooms, designing and teaching lessons and struggling with ways to present ideas, prepare lessons, or assist individual students who have difficulty understanding math. Today, with the use of technology, we are able to collaborate with colleagues to plan lessons, to reflect on problems, and to explore solutions.

Technology is a time saver. Elementary teachers have always spent long hours creating materials for classroom math activities. We have cut and colored and pasted to create activities to help our students explore and review math skills. Instead of searching in stores for flash cards or creating our own with index cards, we can now print out sets in any size with any math facts simply by going to a website (e.g., www.aplusmath.com, www.edHelper.com). Rather than creating paper-and-pencil tasks to review math vocabulary, crossword puzzles can be created with key vocabulary from a site (e.g., www.puzzle maker.com). Instead of creating 30 different math vocabulary bingo cards, we can download cards tailored to any number of math lessons (e.g., www.teachingmadeeasy.com). Teachers can create printable worksheets specific to their students' skills by going to the www.edHelper.com website. Technology has placed resources for constructing math activities at our fingertips.

Technology has also reduced the time needed for lesson planning and recordkeeping. Many websites have ideas for particular lessons and offer a variety of teacher tools and creative lesson ideas (e.g., www.math.com, www.abcteach.com). Some sites direct us to others such as www.sitesforteachers.com. Web searches can locate information on any topic just by plugging key words into search engines (e.g., www.google.com, www.yahoo.com). We can get support in developing rubrics from www.rubistar.4teachers.org. Sample lesson plans written by teachers are available at various sites (e.g., www.lessonplanz.com); we can share our ideas or ask for help from other teachers through discussion strands (e.g., www.proteacher.com).

Technology brings professional development to teachers in all shapes and sizes. We can visit classrooms and see instruction in progress on CD-ROMs (e.g., the *NCTM Navigation* series). Online courses are available to expand our teaching skills. Seminars and coursework can be found at sites such as www.mathsolutions.com and www.ber.org.

We can access professional literature to enhance our teaching skills from www.heine-mann.com or purchase teacher resource books from www.teacherspecialty.com. Websites allow us to connect with professional organizations, to chat with others about concerns, or to share our experiences. The Internet allows us to access up-to-the-minute professional articles and research. Through technology, an endless amount of information to enhance teaching and to help us grow as professionals is available at the touch of the keys.

What Are Some Things to Consider When Using Technology in the Classroom?

Despite the many benefits of incorporating technology into education, there are still some valid questions and concerns that should be addressed. Students have various levels of knowledge and ability to access technology; many websites are inappropriate for students; many teachers lack a comfort level or expertise in the use of technology; and the cost of purchasing hardware, software, and properly maintaining technology can be prohibitive.

The goal should be equitable access to technology for all students. Teachers can ensure that during the school day they have equal access to technology tools. If schools are equipped with computer labs, then all students can participate in computer activities at the same time; however, in some schools each classroom may be equipped with only a few computers. In these classrooms, managing students' computer time and instituting a system to ensure that they all get a turn with a classroom computer is essential. Some teachers schedule students for a specific time to work on the computer, and others set up a rotation to ensure that each student receives a turn (see Figure 10.3). Time limits are often set for computer use (i.e., students either complete a specified activity or work for a specified amount of time). Teachers might consider computer buddies so that students with limited experience with computers will each have a

FIGURE 10.3   Students enjoy working at computer workstations to explore math skills.

buddy to help them develop their skills. When designing homework, teachers need to consider whether students have home access to technology and be certain an assignment will not put students who do not have access to a computer at home at a disadvantage.

Computers and calculators need to be properly maintained and appropriately used to withstand the wear and tear of classroom use. Students should be taught the proper use of all technology tools. There should be consistent consequences for students who misuse technology, the most reasonable and relevant consequence being the loss of the privilege to use the technology for that day. Teachers might designate several students to clean computer equipment by dusting and covering it for overnight or weekends. Student helpers might periodically check calculators to be sure that all are functioning properly.

Access to websites should be carefully monitored because many are inappropriate for elementary students. Computers should be positioned in such a way that teachers can clearly see monitors.

Many teachers need support for integrating technology into their classrooms. Along with the purchase of classroom equipment, schools and districts should provide training in its use, time for teachers to develop their expertise with the various tools, as well as ideas for integrating technology into classroom lessons. Professional development opportunities should include training, time to practice with the equipment, and technical support as needed. Teachers also will benefit from having a mentor, having opportunities for reflection on the use of instructional technology, and ongoing encouragement (Apple 1995).

All teachers need to have access to technology, and its use and potential should be demonstrated to those who might feel uncomfortable and/or hesitant. The National Council of Teachers of Mathematics (2003) recommends that all schools provide access to computers, calculators, and the Internet; that preservice and inservice teachers receive training in the use of instructional technology; and that technology be integrated into lessons delivery and student assessment.

CLASSROOM IDEAS
Quick and Easy Calculator Activities

The following activities will give students practice using the calculator in addition to providing practice with their numeration and mental math skills.

Counting Up or Back

Have students practice their counting skills by counting forward or backward from a designated number. Have them record their guess for the next number and then use the calculator to check the guess. For example:

- Start at 24. Count forward by tens.
- Start at 359. Count forward by hundreds.
- Start at 46,798. Count forward by thousands.
- Start at 325. Count backward by tens.
- Start at 4,678. Count backward by hundreds.
- Start at 175,204. Count backward by thousands.

Flip It

Try this riddle game as students are learning how to enter numbers into the calculator. If numbers are entered correctly, the answer to the riddle should appear on the display when the calculator is turned upside-down. Here are some possible riddles.

Clue: What we scramble for breakfast.
Enter: Nine hundred, ninety-three

Clue: It rings to tell us school is starting.
Enter: Seven thousand, seven hundred, thirty-eight

Clue: A dog has four of these.
Enter: Five thousand, nine hundred, thirty-seven

When certain numbers are flipped upside-down, they create the following letters on the display: 0-O; 1-i, l; 3-E; 4-h; 5-S; 6-g; 7-L; 8-B; 9-G. Note that some are uppercase and some are lowercase letters, but that's part of the fun in figuring out the missing word! Just create words that use these letters and you're ready to go!

Variation: Older students might be asked to create words and riddles for other students to solve.

Mystery Numbers

To work on patterning and number sense, have students skip-count using the constant function of the calculator (see page 95) and try to find the mystery number.

Skip-count by 30s
I am between 130 and 160.
My tens digit is 5.

Skip-count by 20s
I am between 210 and 240.
My tens digit is 2.

Skip-count by 300s.
I am greater than 4400.
I am less than 5000.
My hundreds digit is 5.

The Range Game

This game supports the development of number sense and provides practice with multiplication skills (Reys et al. 1979). Students are given a range (e.g., between 300 and 450) and asked to find a number that, when multiplied by 45 (or any number you choose), will have a product in that range. Students use their calculators to find a number that will work. Students might be chal-

CLASSROOM IDEAS (continued)
Quick and Easy Calculator Activities

lenged to find the smallest number that works, the largest number that works, or all numbers that work. The range or factor can be made simpler or more complex to match the ability levels of students.

Estimate and Solve

Try some of the following word problems for calculator practice. Encourage students to estimate answers before calculating.

- If there were 4 bears in the park and every day 3 more bears appeared, how many bears would there be in 6 days?
- Brad collected baseball cards. He had 14 cards to start. If he bought 5 cards every day, how many cards would he have after 7 days?
- If Joe had 2 dollars and every day his money doubled, how much money would he have in 10 days?

Summary

Technology helps everyone better express ideas, access information, and communicate with others. Students benefit from engaging in the use of multimedia presentations, opportunities to explore complex tasks with the assistance of technology, learning about more exciting ways to report information, and opportunities to investigate math topics through simulations and interactive activities. Teachers benefit from using technology to assist in planning lessons and researching information; to individualize instruction for students with various ability levels; to quickly and easily communicate with students, parents, and colleagues; and to create presentations that bring math to life for students.

Suggested Resources

Apple Classrooms of Tomorrow. 1995. *Changing the Conversation About Teaching, Learning and Technology: A Report on Ten Years of ACOT Research.* Cupertino, CA: Apple Computer, Inc.

Culp, Katie McMillan, Margaret Honey, and Ellen Mandinach. 2003. *A Retrospective of Twenty Years of Education Technology Policy.* New York: Center for Children and Technology.

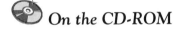

On the CD-ROM

Appendix L—"Must-See" Math Websites

Questions for Reflection

1. How can technology enhance students' understanding of math concepts? Give examples to support your answer.
2. In what ways can the use of technology support teacher planning?
3. What are the benefits of calculator use? Disadvantages?
4. How can you provide opportunities for students to develop mental math, computation, as well as calculator skills?
5. Search for some math websites to support your teaching; share a few with your colleagues.

Fey, James T., ed. 1992. *Calculators in Mathematics Education: 1992 Yearbook of the National Council of Teachers of Mathematics*. Reston, VA: National Council of Teachers of Mathematics.

National Council of Teachers of Mathematics. 2003. *NCTM Position Statement: The Use of Technology in the Learning and Teaching of Mathematics*. Reston, VA: National Council of Teachers of Mathematics.

Reys, Robert, Barbara Bestgen, Terrence Coburn, Harold Schoen, Richard Shumway, Charlotte Wheatley, Grayson Wheatley, and Arthur White. 1979. *Keystrokes: Multiplication and Division*. Palo Alto, CA: Creative Publications.

CHAPTER ELEVEN

Maximizing Parent Involvement

Much attention has been paid to the benefits of parents' involvement in their children's education. Although parents frequently read to them at home and understand its value in developing their literacy skills, they are often uncomfortable doing math with their children or even knowing what types of math to do. Many parents have had negative experiences with mathematics while in school, and many others do not understand the changes in today's math classrooms. Parents and teachers working together strengthen the education offered to students. This chapter focuses on the potential role of parents (or home caregivers) in the mathematics education of their children and identifies strategies to strengthen that role.

What Is Parent Involvement?

Parent involvement can mean many different things; it can be simple communication with the school, attendance at school functions, volunteering in the classroom, or actively helping children with math at home. There are many ways for parents to be involved in their children's education. It is important to allow parents to choose a type of involvement with which they are comfortable. With many demands on parents' time and energy, some are able to offer their time and assistance in school while others can only offer their children encouragement and support at home. Helping each parent understand the importance of being involved in his or her child's education, and helping to find a unique way to support the child is the ultimate goal.

Why Involve Parents in Children's Math Education?

"Some parents and other authority figures, as well as societal influences like the media, convey the message that not everyone is expected to be successful in mathematics and thus that disengagement from school mathematics is acceptable" (NCTM 2000, 372). It is critical that students believe they can do math and that parents recognize their influence on that belief. Even those parents who are reluctant to volunteer in classrooms, or feel ill-prepared to support their children in learning specific math skills, can be encouraged to show confidence in students' abilities and to model a positive attitude about the role of math in their lives.

Involving parents in their children's math education fosters positive attitudes toward mathematics and enhances motivation (Edge 2000, Secada 2002). Parents have a powerful influence on their children, and those who are anxious about mathematics or unable to value the importance of math skills can pass the attitudes on to them. Parent involvement in school helps to counter stereotypes about mathematics that are often passed from parent to child (e.g., the belief that some people can do math and others just can't). The more parents understand math, feel confident in their own ability with math, and understand the importance of passing on positive messages about math, the more positive and confident students will become.

Studies have shown a positive relationship between parent involvement and student success in school (Edge 2000, Goldstein and Campbell 1991, Peressini 2000, Stallings and Stipek 1986, Tangri and Moles 1987). Student success as a result of parent involvement in schools has been defined in a variety of ways including less absenteeism, improved achievement, and higher rates of completing school and becoming employed.

Involving parents in informal home activities to support their children's understanding of math has been shown to have positive effects (Goldstein and Campbell 1991) even for busy parents or those who may be poorly educated (Tangri and Moles 1987). One-on-one assistance with math skills can be a valuable help to students who need to talk through ideas as they struggle to develop their understanding. In the *Math Pairs: Parents as Partners Program*, parents (or other home helpers) were introduced to problem-solving strategies and became problem-solving buddies with their children as students explored a set of weekly problems. Parents were coached in ways to talk students through their thinking. The results of the study indicated that the students with home partners showed greater improvement in problem-solving skills than those who worked alone on the problems (O'Connell 1992). In addition, parents who participated in the program showed more confidence in their own abilities and a greater understanding of school math priorities.

Parental involvement in mathematics enhances the home–school connection and allows them to see the ways in which math is taught to their children. They become involved in their children's education and play a role in strengthening their math achievement and attitudes toward math. It also strengthens the relationship between parents and teachers through communication about and awareness of math priorities and instructional strategies. Parents' involvement assists teachers by providing a ready resource for helping students as they build math understandings.

Can Teachers Help Parents Understand Math Priorities in Today's Classrooms?

Math has changed since many of us were in school. Teachers have come to appreciate the changes and the benefits they bring to today's students as they focus on understanding and application rather than just rote skills. Unlike us, the parents of most students have not had the time to reflect on these changes. They know how they were taught math and may be comfortable helping students with basic computations, but often are pulled from their comfort zone by many of the math tasks posed to their children today. It is important to gently, but firmly, help parents understand the changes in mathematics and the reasons for those changes. As parents' awareness is built, we will be more likely to receive their support because our shared purpose is to help their children become confident and competent mathematicians.

Schools and districts can help parents understand today's math priorities through programs, such as Family Math Nights or PTA-sponsored events, that focus on mathematics teaching and learning. Teachers can keep parents aware of math activities and objectives through newsletters, websites, emails, and discussions at Back-to-School Nights. Communicating with parents is key to helping them better understand and support school math programs. Our goal is to help parents see that children who learn to "do" math rather than understand math will be at a disadvantage (Mokros 1996).

How Can Teachers Make Parents Aware of Current Math Practices and Priorities?

Within schools and classrooms, it is important to develop a system to communicate with parents about mathematics. "Families become advocates for education standards when they understand the importance of a high-quality mathematics education for their children" (NCTM 2000, 378). School bulletins, classroom newsletters, and school and teacher websites are wonderful ways to open communication about mathematics.

Many schools have bulletins or newsletters that go home to parents on a weekly or monthly basis. Often there is a section on nutrition or counseling or reading to make parents aware of pertinent information; consider including a math section in the school's newsletter. Just small quotes about math or tips to help students at home will begin to make parents aware of math standards and ways that they can support their children's development of math skills. Maybe select a tip from *Helping Your Child Learn Math* (Kanter and Darby 1999), available through the U.S. Department of Education, which contains enough practical ideas to last throughout the school year. Classroom newsletters can provide the same types of practical ideas but can be grade-level specific and connect the tips to the current topic being studied in class.

Websites have become a wonderful way to communicate with parents. School sites can offer links to math websites that might provide parents with ideas about math standards or tips for working with their children (see Appendix L for some parent website links). Classroom websites can highlight topics being studied and lesson objectives, point out children's literature to read at home to support a math concept, highlight homework policies and explain homework activities, present calendars with due dates for assignments, suggest home activities to support a concept, and provide links to additional websites.

The widespread use of email facilitates quick communication between parents and teachers. Teachers with websites can provide a link to their email from the site, and even teachers without websites will see the ease of communicating electronically when sending quick updates about students' progress. Email also allows parents to easily notify teachers of concerns or to ask for clarification on assignments. Early in the year, teachers can send an introductory email to parents to initiate communication. A group email or listserv allows teachers to send quick reminders or bits of information to all parents with one simple note. Remember, all parents may not have email capabilities, so any communication that must be seen by all parents will still need to be sent in a more traditional way.

Prior to beginning a mathematics unit or topic, many teachers send home parent letters about it. Many textbook companies provide such letters as a supplement to texts. The letters are meant to inform parents about the upcoming topic, highlight key concepts, and suggest ways to support their children at home. Whether using textbook-designed letters or creating them, sending unit letters helps keep parents informed of the classroom's latest math activities.

Some schools establish a parent lending library; including books that support home learning in math are great additions to such a library. The *Family Math* series from the University of California contains practical, easy-to-use guides for home activities and would be a perfect addition to a parent lending library.

When developing newsletters, websites, or parent letters, remember the importance of providing some tips or information for non-English speaking parents. Perhaps parent volunteers or bilingual school staff would be willing to provide assistance in this area. Even students who are beginning to speak English at school may have parents who do not speak English at home. It is important that those parents also understand the math program and know ways to assist their children. School or district ESL (i.e., English as a second language) specialists can provide ideas and assistance for interacting with non-English speaking parents.

How Can Teachers Encourage Parent–Child Home Activities?

A foundation for home activities is an environment in which students and families value math and are willing to talk about it. Helping parents understand the value of talking about mathematics is a good place to start. Mokros (1996) suggests telling parents to verbalize when using math at home, to talk aloud about measuring a window for curtains or following a recipe. An environment in which math is valued and students are praised for their abilities will open up lots of possibilities for math discussions and explorations. Helping parents see that math is a way of thinking, not a right answer, may help them see math discussions as a way to develop thinking even if wrong answers emerge along the way. Helping parents see that math is about discovery will help them model positive behaviors and instill positive attitudes within their children.

Parents often need help in understanding their role in supporting math instruction, as well as practical ideas for ways to enhance their children's abilities. The more they know about math instruction in class, the better able they will be to support their children at home. Some home support may take the form of occasional assistance as children experience difficulty with an idea and just need to talk it over with someone. Other support might be ongoing support for students who need extra help on a regular basis. Opening up discussions with parents and offering ideas for working with their children at home will provide students with needed support and assistance.

Parent conference times are great opportunities to share ideas about ways to support and assist children at home. Try to limit suggestions to one or two ideas targeted to a student's specific needs. The more precise the suggestions, the easier it will be for parents to follow through with the ideas. If suggesting helping a child with basic facts, provide an activity or two that would target that skill (e.g., a card game that works on basic facts). Always include the importance of positive interactions and encouraging words. Unpleasant parent–child experiences will not help the student progress with her or his skills.

To become comfortable engaging in parent–child home activities, parents may not only need ideas for the activities but also materials for them and an understanding of the goals of the activities. Parent–child activity programs should provide a variety of home activity ideas and an explanation as to why the activities are important for developing math skills. This information can be shared in various ways including websites, newsletters, parent evenings at school, and/or discussions at parent conference time.

Buddy programs offer parents and children opportunities work together on home math activities, which may be sent home weekly or monthly. Tasks can vary depending on grade level or math topic. Primary-level parent–child activities might include reading a book and drawing a picture about the math in the story; or counting specific objects seen during a car trip; or creating patterns with marshmallows, raisins, or peanuts. Intermediate-level tasks might include creating designs with toothpicks and trying to explain them to each other using math words, or estimating the area of a room and measuring to see how close the estimate was, or using grocery ads to plan a party menu and then determining the cost for the food. Buddy activities should be fun and engaging for both parents and children. Directions should be clear and materials should be provided if they are unavailable in the home. Tasks should not be lengthy and the frequency of the tasks should respect parents' busy lives. Participation should not be required, but encouraged. If parents are not available or willing to participate, older siblings might become partners for activities.

How Can Parents Provide Support for Students' Homework?

Parents often see homework help as the way they can be involved with students' math education. Unfortunately, many negative behaviors and attitudes can surface when parents help children with homework. Discuss the importance of being encouraging and helping reduce their children's anxiety. Discuss why the process is as important as the answer. Allow parents to communicate with you about students' struggles with homework and be willing to adapt assignments that are causing extreme anxiety or frustration.

Homework has traditionally been viewed as a way to reinforce and practice skills taught in class, but consider the use of it to push students to think further about ideas or to pose questions that can lead into classroom activities. Could parents and students discuss the ways in which they use fractions every day or the ways in which they need to measure or estimate in daily life? Would these types of discussions focus students on the meaningfulness of the skills they are learning and help parents feel more confident and positive about their abilities to connect with their children as they talk about math?

What Types of Schoolwide Activities Can Promote Parent Involvement?

Special programs that bring parents into schools offer great opportunities to promote awareness of mathematics initiatives. Back-to-School Night is probably the most highly attended evening event because parents come to school to learn about the coming year and to meet their children's new teachers. As teachers meet parents and present an overview of the coming year, providing some insights into what will be taught in mathematics, as well as how it will be taught, will pave the way for better understanding as students move through the curriculum. Teachers might display math manipulatives or resource books so that parents have an opportunity to see instructional materials, and providing parents with a list of skills and standards is also a good practice. Mentioning the importance of basic skills will relieve many parents' minds, but mentioning the importance of thinking and problem-solving skills and students' understanding of computation skills is also an important point to make. Help parents understand that the goal is for students to know the basics *and* be able to understand and apply the basics.

Many schools also help parents understand mathematics instruction by inviting them to participate in special math programs. Programs might be for parents only and can offer an opportunity for them to hear about the changes in math instruction and to engage in some activities to help them appreciate the need for the changes. Many parents will readily admit that they mastered the basics but struggled with problem-solving activities or more complex areas of mathematics that demanded an understanding of the skills they had memorized. Help parents recognize that the goal is to support their children in learning math without the anxiety many of them experienced and to give their children the understanding to apply skills to increasingly complex problems.

Evening or weekend math programs that engage parents and children in exploring math together are very popular and help parents experience math in a new way. Family Math Nights are programs in which parents and children share an evening of math activities. A parent and child might move through stations in a series of self-directed explorations, or they might participate in teacher- or volunteer-directed activities in which they explore a variety of mathematical ideas. The evenings offer hands-on activities (e.g., probability investigations, data collection and analysis, exploration of geometry concepts through tangram or pattern block activities, or card games to explore fraction or decimal concepts). Family Math Nights promote parent–child involvement, create an awareness of math strategies and standards, stimulate excitement for mathematics, and nurture positive attitudes about mathematics.

Math Fairs are a way for students to display projects and for parents to see the diverse ways in which math touches students' lives. Students choose projects that connect to their math interests and may work alone or with a partner. Projects are displayed at an evening gathering and families can view many children's projects as they take special pride in the work of their own children. Student projects might include designing math board games, creating and labeling various geometric shapes, designing and conducting a survey and graphing the results, creating a tessellation, designing a logic matrix problem, conducting a probability experiment, or designing a series of patterns. Math Fairs allow students to choose an activity that matches their interests and highlights the varied applications of mathematics.

Math carnivals are active events in which children engage in math at various booths or stations. Students score points, earn ribbons, receive prizes, or just have fun as they participate in a variety of math-related events, such as the long jump, in which they measure the length of their jumps. Students might be challenged to estimate how long it will take them to complete an obstacle course, or try to toss bean bags into geometric shapes marked in chalk on the playground pavement. They might fish for (and solve) math facts by plucking plastic ducks, with math facts written underneath, from a pond. Traditional carnival games like tossing rings, throwing darts, or guessing age or weight can all be adapted to the math theme. Math Carnivals are fun and active, and focus on math skills from measurement to money to geometry to basic facts.

CLASSROOM IDEAS
Quick and Easy Parent Involvement Ideas

Interactive Open House

If the school holds an Open House for parents to visit during the school day, plan an interactive activity for which they are invited to sit alongside their children and participate. Rather than the traditional experience of standing along the fringes of the classroom and watching children do math, parents can be engaged in playing games to review basic facts or use geoboards to explore symmetry or solve logic puzzles. The activities will be fun and may give them insight into ways they might work with their children at home.

Family Game Night

Suggest a Family Game Night and provide parents with ideas about some common games that require students to use math skills. Younger students might practice comparing whole numbers as they play the card game War, extend their understanding of spatial relationships as they build with blocks, develop their logical reasoning skills by playing checkers, or practice their counting skills as they move a certain number of spaces in simple board games. Older students can apply their money skills to play Monopoly; use their understanding of coordinate

CLASSROOM IDEAS (continued)
Quick and Easy Parent Involvement Ideas

graphs to play Battleship; or apply their logical reasoning skills to play Connect Four, Chess, or Mastermind.

Read Math
Send home a list of children's books that support the math ideas being explored in class. Encourage parents to read with their children and then discuss the math from the story. For math literature sorted by topic, see Appendix D.

Math Backpacks
Develop some take-home kits for students to check out for parent–child use. Backpacks should contain materials and directions for a hands-on activity. They might contain a small clock with moveable hands and some cards with various times for students to show on the clock, or a ruler and a list of items to estimate and then measure, or a tangram and some pictures of tangrams arranged in animal shapes for parent and child to try to

replicate. When students return the backpack, they may sign out another one.

Math Interviews
Involve students in talking to their parents about the math they use each day at home and at work. Students might be asked to interview them and report to the class on the ways in which their parents use math. Primary students might just gather general information, but intermediate students will want to gather information on parents' use of fractions, decimals, measurement, money, and/or geometry. Parents may be surprised at the many ways they use math, and students will gain insights into the applicability of the math they are learning.

Math Websites for Parents
There are many websites that supply parents with information on mathematics, as well as ideas for home activities. Websites can also provide homework help for students. For a list of websites to share with parents, see Appendix L.

Summary

Schools and students benefit when parents are involved in education. Parents can get involved in a variety of ways. Parents can become informed about math activities or standards through websites or newsletters, support their children through home activities, or participate in schoolwide math events. Welcoming parents into schools and classrooms helps them better understand the

math being taught, provides them with ideas for helping their children, and helps promote a positive attitude toward mathematics.

 ## On the CD-ROM

Appendix D—Children's Literature Related to Math Concepts
Appendix K—Math Centers
Appendix L—"Must-See" Math Websites

Questions for Reflection

1. What does your school do to encourage parent involvement in math? What do you do as a teacher to involve parents in math?

2. What is your goal for involving parents? At what level would you like them to be involved?

3. Why is it important to inform parents about the math being studied in school?

4. In what ways can technology enhance communication with parents? Give examples of some information or issues that can be communicated to parents in an electronic format to enhance the math program.

5. What if a parent does not feel comfortable helping his or her child with math? In what ways can you support the parent?

Suggested Resources

Appleman, Maya, and Julie King. 1993. *Exploring Everyday Math: Ideas for Students, Teachers, and Parents*. Portsmouth, NH: Heinemann.

Coates, Grace Davila, and Jean Kerr Stenmark. 1997. *Family Math for Young Children*. Berkeley: Regents of the University of California.

Coates, Grace Davila, and Virginia Thompson. 2003. *Family Math II: Achieving Success in Mathematics*. Berkeley: Regents of the University of California.

Kanter, Patsy F., and Linda B. Darby. 1999. *Helping Your Child Learn Math*. Jessup, MD: U.S. Department of Education (Available at www.ed.gov/pubs/parents/Math/index.html.)

Mokros, Jan. 1996. *Beyond Facts and Flashcards: Exploring Math with Your Kids*. Portsmouth, NH: Heinemann.

Stenmark, Jean Kerr, Virginia Thompson, and Ruth Cossey. 1986. *Family Math*. Berkeley: Regents of the University of California.

Parent Videotape

Burns, Marilyn. 1994. *Mathematics: What Are You Teaching My Child?* White Plains, NY: Scholastic.

Conclusion

Many of us experienced very traditional teaching methods in our elementary mathematics classrooms. My classroom experiences led me to a series of misinformed beliefs about mathematics. Reflecting on my experiences, and the experiences of my students, has led me to change my beliefs about mathematics and to rethink the ways in which I teach it.

Through changing our instructional practices, we can guide students to a healthier understanding of mathematics. We can help them develop positive attitudes toward mathematics and help them feel confident in their math abilities. We can assist them in developing understanding rather than settling for rote memory. We can nurture their appreciation for exploration and discovery, and can help them value even wrong answers that may lead them to new insights.

The first step is to reflect on our instructional practices and the impact of those practices on students' mathematical thinking. Through reflecting on current practices and being open to new ideas, we can begin to modify our teaching to incorporate more thinking, more talking, and more reasoning. We can find ways to build on our many strengths and add to our repertoire of instructional practices. We can discover ways to strengthen our teaching by learning more about how children learn mathematics, then expanding on the practices we use to teach mathematics.

Some teachers enjoy taking university classes and/or participating in workshops and seminars, while others prefer to explore professional literature. Many schools have book study groups in which teachers read professional literature and discuss it with their colleagues. Professional development workshops help us gather new ideas, and interactions with colleagues help us recognize the different approaches that can lead to math success. Although we may not all agree on how to pursue professional growth, we recognize the need to further develop our understanding of math teaching and learning. Our reflections through professional development will help us with the construction of a new model of what a math teacher should do and say and teach.

Changing math for our students begins with changing ideas about math within ourselves. As we reflect on what we want for students, our vision of an effective teacher of mathematics becomes clearer.

- We begin to recognize the importance of teacher questioning to guide our students' understanding.

- We become open to new strategies that will engage our students in writing about mathematics.

▊ We begin to recognize that differentiation makes sense and that teaching math in one way to all students cannot meet their individual needs.

▊ We concede that problem solving is the reason we teach basic skills and therefore must be a major focus in our classrooms.

▊ We begin to hone the skills necessary to integrate materials such as children's literature and manipulatives into our lessons in meaningful ways.

▊ We begin to see the critical role parents can play in facilitating student success and why our classrooms should be open to them.

▊ We acknowledge that students develop understanding when engaged in math talk with peers.

▊ We explore options for increasing constructive math talk in our classrooms.

▊ We accept the responsibility for developing our own and students' technology skills in order to enhance teaching and support learning.

We need to bring the power of mathematics to all students by engaging them in our lessons and supporting them as they develop understanding. Math classrooms must be places where students are doers and talkers and thinkers, and where there is less silence and more talk. Rather than just "doing" math, our students should be exploring, conjecturing, testing, explaining, justifying, and ultimately *understanding and valuing* mathematics.

We can choose to have a math classroom in which students memorize facts, formulas, and procedures, or a math classroom in which students explore and develop an understanding of mathematics. Through our reflections about our teaching and our understanding of our goals, we can ensure that our students' experiences will lead them to truer beliefs about mathematics and its role in their lives.

We must go beyond how we were taught and teach how we wish we had been taught. We must bring to life a vision of what a mathematics classroom should be. (Lindquist et al. 1992, v)

References

AIMS Educational Foundation. 1987. *Primarily Bears*. Fresno, CA: AIMS Educational Foundation.

Andrini, Beth. 1991. *Cooperative Learning and Mathematics*. Capistrano, CA: Resources for Teachers.

Apple Classrooms of Tomorrow. 1995. *Changing the Conversation About Teaching, Learning and Technology: A Report on Ten Years of ACOT Research*. Cupertino, CA: Apple Computer, Inc.

Appleman, Maya, and Julie King. 1993. *Exploring Everyday Math: Ideas for Students, Teachers, and Parents*. Portsmouth, NH: Heinemann.

Artzt, Alice F., and Claire M. Newman. 1990. *How to Use Cooperative Learning in the Mathematics Class*. Reston, VA: National Council of Teachers of Mathematics.

Bloomer, Anne, and Phyllis Carlson. 1992. *Activity Math: Using Manipulatives in the Classroom*. Lebanon, IN: Pearson Education.

Braddon, Kathryn L., Nancy J. Hall, and Dale Taylor. 1993. *Math Through Children's Literature*. Englewood, CO: Teacher Ideas Press.

Bransford, John D., Ann L. Brown, and Rodney R. Cocking, eds. 1999. *How People Learn: Brain, Mind, Experience, and School*. Washington, DC: National Academy Press.

Bresser, Rusty. 1995. *Math and Literature, Grades 4–6*. Sausalito, CA: Math Solutions Publications.

Burns, Marilyn. 1992a. *About Teaching Mathematics, A K–8 Resource: Second Edition*. Sausalito, CA: Math Solutions Publications.

———. 1992b. *Math and Literature (K–3) Book One*. Sausalito, CA: Math Solutions Publications.

———. 1995. *Writing in Math Class: A Resource for Grades K–8*. Sausalito, CA: Math Solutions Publications.

———. 2002. *Mathematics Teaching for Understanding* (videotapes). Vernon Hills, IL: ETA/Cuisenaire.

Carpenter, Thomas P., Elizabeth Fennema, Megan Loef Franke, Linda Levi, and Susan B. Empson. 1999. *Children's Mathematics: Cognitively Guided Instruction.* Portsmouth, NH: Heinemann.

Carpenter, Thomas P., Megan Loef Franke, and Linda Levi. 2003. *Thinking Mathematically: Integrating Arithmetic and Algebra in Elementary School.* Portsmouth, NH: Heinemann.

Carpenter, Thomas P., and Thomas A. Romberg. 2004. *Powerful Practices in Mathematics and Science.* Madison: The Board of Regents of the University of Wisconsin (CD-ROM and monograph).

Chapin, Suzanne H., Catherine O'Connor, and Nancy Canavan Anderson. 2003. *Classroom Discussions: Using Math Talk to Help Students Learn.* Sausalito, CA: Math Solutions Publications.

Clements, Douglas H., and Sue McMillen. 2002. "Rethinking Concrete Manipulatives." In *Putting Research into Practice in the Elementary Grades,* edited by Donald L. Chambers. Reston, VA: National Council of Teachers of Mathematics.

Coates, Grace Davila, and Jean Kerr Stenmark. 1997. *Family Math for Young Children.* Berkeley: Regents of the University of California.

Coates, Grace Davila, and Virginia Thompson. 2003. *Family Math II: Achieving Success in Mathematics.* Berkeley: Regents of the University of California.

Collins C., and J. N. Mangieri, eds. 1992. *Teaching Thinking: An Agenda for the Twenty-First Century.* Hillsdale, NJ: Erlbaum.

Cooper, J. David. 2000. *Literacy: Helping Children Construct Meaning.* Boston: Houghton Mifflin.

Corwin, Rebecca B. 1996. *Talking Mathematics—Supporting Children's Voices.* Portsmouth, NH: Heinemann.

Culp, Katie McMillan, Margaret Honey, and Ellen Mandinach. 2003. *A Retrospective of Twenty Years of Education Technology Policy.* New York: Center for Children and Technology.

DeBolt, Virginia. 1998. *Write! Mathematics.* San Clemente, CA: Kagan Cooperative Learning.

Edge, Douglas, ed. 2000. *Involving Parents in Mathematics Education.* Reston, VA: National Council of Teachers of Mathematics.

Erickson, Tim. 1989. *Get It Together—Math Problems for Groups (Grades 4–12).* Berkeley: Regents of the University of California.

Fennema, Elizabeth, Thomas P. Carpenter, and Susan J. Lamon, eds. 1991. *Integrating Research on Teaching and Learning Mathematics.* Albany: State University of New York Press.

Fennema, Elizabeth, and Thomas A. Romberg. 1999. *Mathematics Classrooms that Promote Understanding.* Mahwah, NJ: Erlbaum.

Fey, James T., ed. 1992. *Calculators in Mathematics Education: 1992 Yearbook of the National Council of Teachers of Mathematics.* Reston, VA: National Council of Teachers of Mathematics.

Forsten, Char, Jim Grant, and Betty Hollas. 2002. *Differentiated Instruction: Different Strategies for Different Learners.* Peterborough, NH: Crystal Springs Books.

Fosnot, Catherine Twomey, and Maarten Dolk. 2002. *Young Mathematicians at Work: Constructing Fractions, Decimals, and Percents.* Portsmouth, NH: Heinemann.

Gall, M. D. 1984. "Synthesis of Research on Teachers' Questioning." *Educational Leadership* 42: 707–24.

Gardner, Howard. 1993. *Multiple Intelligences: The Theory in Practice.* New York: Basic Books.

Goldstein, Sue, and Frances A. Campbell. 1991. "Parents: A Ready Resource." *Arithmetic Teacher* 38 (6): 124–27.

Griffiths, Rachel, and Margaret Clyne. 1991. *Books You Can Count On.* Portsmouth, NH: Heinemann.

———. 1994. *Language in the Mathematics Classroom.* Portsmouth, NH: Heinemann.

Hancock, Vicki, and Frank Betts. 1994. "From the Lagging to the Leading Edge." *Educational Leadership* 51 (7): 24–29.

Hargreaves, Andy, and Michael Fullan. 1998. *What's Worth Fighting for Out There?* New York: Teachers College Press.

Hechtman, Judi, Deborah Ellermeyer, and Sandra Ford Grove. 1998. *Teaching Math with Favorite Picture Books.* New York: Scholastic.

Heibert, James, Thomas P. Carpenter, Elizabeth Fennema, Karen C. Fuson, Diana Wearne, Hanlie Murray, Alwyn Olivier, and Piet Human. 1997. *Making Sense: Teaching and Learning Mathematics with Understanding.* Portsmouth, NH: Heinemann.

Hembree, Ray, and Donald J. Dessart. 1992. "Research on Calculators in Mathematic Education." In *Calculators in Mathematics Education: 1992 Yearbook of the National Council of Teachers of Mathematics,* edited by James T. Fey, 24–26. Reston, VA: National Council of Teachers of Mathematics.

Herrell, Adrienne, and Michael Jordan. 2004. *Fifty Strategies for Teaching English Language Learners.* Upper Saddle River, NJ: Pearson Education.

Hong, Haekyung. 1996. "Effects of Mathematics Learning Through Children's Literature on Math Achievement and Dispositional Outcomes." *Early Childhood Research Quarterly* 11 (4): 477–94.

Jennings, Clara M., James E. Jennings, Joyce Richey, and Lisbeth Dixon-Krauss. 1992. "Increasing Interest and Achievement in Mathematics Through Children's Literature." *Early Childhood Research Quarterly* 7 (2): 263–76.

Johnson, D. W., and R. T. Johnson. 1999. *Learning Together and Alone: Cooperative, Competitive, and Individualistic Learning.* Boston: Allyn and Bacon.

Kagan, Spencer. 1992. *Cooperative Learning.* San Clemente, CA: Resources for Teachers.

Kanter, Patsy F., and Linda B. Darby. 1999. *Helping Your Child Learn Math.* Jessup, MD: U.S. Department of Education.

Keene, Ellin, and Susan Zimmermann. 1997. *Mosaic of Thought: Teaching Comprehension in a Reader's Workshop.* Portsmouth, NH: Heinemann.

Kilpatrick, Jeremy, Jane Swafford, and Bradford Findell, eds. 2001. *Adding It Up: Helping Children Learn Mathematics.* Washington, DC: National Academy Press.

Krpan, Cathy Marks. 2001. *The Write Math: Writing in the Math Class.* Parsippany, NJ: Dale Seymour.

Leinwand, Steven. 2000. *Sensible Mathematics: A Guide for School Leaders.* Portsmouth, NH: Heinemann.

Lester, Frank K., and Randall I. Charles, eds. 2003. *Teaching Mathematics Through Problem Solving: Prekindergarten–Grade 6.* Reston, VA: National Council of Teachers of Mathematics.

Lindquist, Mary Montgomery, Jan Luquire, Angela Gardner, and Sandra Shekaramiz. 1992. *NCTM Addenda Series—Making Sense of Data.* Reston, VA: National Council of Teachers of Mathematics.

Ma, Liping. 1999. *Knowing and Teaching Elementary Mathematics.* Mahwah, NJ: Erlbaum.

Marzano, Robert J., Debra J. Pickering, and Jane E. Pollock. 2001. *Classroom Instruction That Works: Research-Based Strategies for Increasing Student Achievement.* Alexandria, VA: Association for Supervision and Curriculum Development.

Miller, Elizabeth. 1998. *Read It! Draw It! Solve It! (Grades K–3)*. Menlo Park, CA: Dale Seymour.

Miller, Marcia, and Martin Lee. 1997. *The Mega-Fun Multiplication Facts Activity Book*. New York: Scholastic.

Mokros, Jan. 1996. *Beyond Facts and Flashcards: Exploring Math with Your Kids*. Portsmouth, NH: Heinemann.

Moore, David W., Sharon Arthur Moore, Patricia M. Cunningham, and James W. Cunningham. 1994. *Developing Readers and Writers in the Content Areas, K–12*. White Plains, NY: Longman.

Murray, Miki. 2004. *Teaching Mathematics Vocabulary in Context*. Portsmouth, NH: Heinemann.

National Research Council. *Everybody Counts*. 1989. Washington, DC: National Academy of Sciences.

National Council of Teachers of Mathematics. 1989. *Curriculum and Evaluation Standards for School Mathematics*. Reston, VA: National Council of Teachers of Mathematics.

———. 1991. *Professional Standards for Teaching Mathematics*. Reston, VA: National Council of Teachers of Mathematics.

———. 1995. *Assessment Standards for School Mathematics*. Reston, VA: National Council of Teachers of Mathematics.

———. 2000. *Principles and Standards for School Mathematics*. Reston, VA: National Council of Teachers of Mathematics.

———. 2003. NCTM *Position Statement: The Use of Technology in the Learning and Teaching of Mathematics*. Reston, VA: National Council of Teachers of Mathematics.

O'Connell, Susan R. 1992. "Math Pairs—Parents as Partners." *Arithmetic Teacher* 40 (1): 10–12.

———. 1997. *Glyphs! Data Communication for Primary Mathematicians*. Grand Rapids, MI: Frank Schaffer Publications.

———. 1998. *Real World Math for Grades 4–6*. Grand Rapids, MI: Frank Schaffer Publications.

———. 2000. *Introduction to Problem Solving: Strategies for the Elementary Math Classroom*. Portsmouth, NH: Heinemann.

———. 2001a. *Math—The Write Way for Grades 2–3*. Grand Rapids, MI: Frank Schaffer Publications.

———. 2001b. *Math—The Write Way for Grades 4–5*. Grand Rapids, MI: Frank Schaffer Publications.

———. 2001c. *Math—The Write Way for Grades 6–7*. Grand Rapids, MI: Frank Schaffer Publications.

Peressini, Dominic D. 2000. "What's All the Fuss About Involving Parents in Mathematics Education?" In *Involving Families in Mathematics Education*, edited by Douglas Edge, 5–10. Reston, VA: National Council of Teachers of Mathematics.

Redfield, D. L., and E. W. Rosseau. 1981. "A Meta-Analysis of Experimental Research on Teacher Questioning Behavior." *Review of Educational Research* 51: 237–45.

Reys, Robert, Barbara Bestgen, Terrence Coburn, Harold Schoen, Richard Shumway, Charlotte Wheatley, Grayson Wheatley, and Arthur White. 1979. *Keystrokes: Multiplication and Division*. Palo Alto, CA: Creative Publications.

Richardson, Kathy. 1999. *Developing Number Concepts: Planning Guide*. Lebanon, IN: Pearson Education.

Rowan, Thomas, and Barbara Bourne. 2001. *Thinking Like Mathematicians: Putting the NCTM Standards into Practice*. Portsmouth, NH: Heinemann.

Sakshaug, Lynae E., Melfried Olson, and Judith Olson. 2002. *Children Are Mathematical Problem Solvers*. Reston, VA: National Council of Teachers of Mathematics.

Secada, Walter G. 2002. "Parental Involvement in a Time of Changing Demographics." In *Putting Research into Practice in the Elementary Grades*, edited by Donald L. Chambers, 302–306. Reston, VA: National Council of Teachers of Mathematics.

Sharp, Janet M., and Karen Bush Hoiberg. 2005. *Learning and Teaching K–8 Mathematics*. Boston: Pearson Education.

Slavin, Robert E. 1983. *Cooperative Learning*. New York: Longman.

Stallings, Jane A., and Deborah Stipek. 1986. "Research on Early Childhood Education and Elementary School Teaching Programs." In *Handbook of Research on Teaching*, edited by Merlin C. Wittrock, 727–53. New York: Macmillan.

Stenmark, Jean Kerr, Virginia Thompson, and Ruth Cossey. 1986. *Family Math*. Berkeley: Regents of the University of California.

Strong, Richard, Ed Thomas, Matthew Perini, and Harvey Silver. 2004. "Creating a Differentiated Mathematics Classroom." *Educational Leadership* (February): 73–78.

Sullivan, Peter, and Pat Lilburn. 2002. *Good Questions for Math Teaching: Why Ask Them and What to Ask, Grades K–6*. Sausalito, CA: Math Solutions Publications.

Tangri, Sandra, and Oliver Moles. 1987. "Parents and the Community." In *Educators' Handbook: A Research Perspective*, edited by Virginia Richardson-Koehler, 519–50. New York: Longman.

Thiessen, Diane. 2004. *Exploring Mathematics Through Literature*. Reston, VA: National Council of Teachers of Mathematics.

Tomlinson, Carol Ann. 2001. *How to Differentiate Instruction in Mixed-Ability Classrooms, Second Edition*. Alexandria, VA: Association for Supervision and Curriculum Development.

Tomlinson, Carol Ann, and Caroline Cunningham Eidson. 2003. *Differentiation in Practice: A Resource Guide for Differentiating Curriculum*. Alexandria, VA: Association for Supervision and Curriculum Development.

Van de Walle, John A. 2004. *Elementary and Middle School Mathematics—Teaching Developmentally*. Boston: Pearson Education.

Welchman-Tischler, Rosamond. 1992. *How to Use Children's Literature to Teach Mathematics*. Reston, VA: National Council of Teachers of Mathematics.

Westley, Joan. 1994. *Puddle Questions: Assessing Mathematical Thinking* (a series with a book for every grade level). Mountain View, CA: Creative Publications.

Wheatley, Grayson H., and Douglas H. Clements. 2002. "Calculators and Constructivism." In *Putting Research into Practice in the Elementary Grades*, edited by Donald L. Chambers, 269–71. Reston, VA: National Council of Teachers of Mathematics.

Whitin, David J., and Robin Cox. 2003. *A Mathematical Passage: Strategies for Promoting Inquiry in Grades 4–6*. Portsmouth, NH: Heinemann.

Whitin, David J., and Sandra Wilde. 1992. *Read Any Good Math Lately? Children's Books for Mathematical Learning, K–6*. Portsmouth, NH: Heinemann.

Whitin, Phyllis, and David J. Whitin. 2000. *Math Is Language Too: Talking and Writing in the Mathematics Classroom*. Urbana, IL: National Council of Teachers of English.

Zike, Dinah. 2003. *Big Book of Math*. San Antonio: Dinah-Might Adventures, LP.